Staying Home
Instead

Staying Home Instead

How to Quit the Working-Mom Rat Race and Survive Financially

by

CHRISTINE DAVIDSON

Lexington Books

D.C. Heath and Company • Lexington, Massachusetts • Toronto

Library of Congress Cataloging-in-Publication Data

Davidson, Christine
Staying home instead.

Bibliography: p.
Includes index.
1. Mothers—Employment—Social aspects—United States.
I. Title.
HD6055.2.U6D38   1986   640'.43'0240431   85-45298
ISBN 0-669-11266-6 (alk. paper)
ISBN 0-669-12878-3 (pbk. : alk. paper)

Published simultaneously in Canada
Printed in the United States of America
Casebound International Standard Book Number: 0-669-11266-6
Paperbound International Standard Book Number: 0-669-12878-3
Library of Congress Catalog Card Number: 85-45298

The paper used in this publication meets
the minimum requirements of American National Standard
for Information Sciences—Permanence of Paper
for Printed Library Materials, ANSI Z39.48-1984.

The last numbers on the right below
indicate the number and date of printing

10 9 8 7 6 5 4 3 2 1

95 94 93 92 91 90 89 88 87 86

For Shirley Goodstone (in memoriam),
Alice K. Boatwright,
and most of all, Chip, Jenny, and Mike.

Contents

Preface

THIS is a book written in support, indeed in loud praise, of stay-at-home mothers. That "stay-at-home mothers" has become a separate designation indicates how much has changed in American family life in the last twenty years. In some ways, this is good: we no longer assume that the majority of women in our society will marry young, have children shortly thereafter, and stay home indefinitely. There are infinite possibilities in work and in life-styles today. But the changes and possibilities have created confusion and suffering too, largely through distorted feminist philosophies and the modern mythology that says happiness for women lies in promotions and money.

Inflation and other economic factors have pressured mothers to go to work today. But so has the success ethic, a warped interpretation of the work ethic that began fading in the 1960s but has been revived by an influential element in the women's movement as well as by the current "yuppie" trend. The connection between the success ethic and mothers working outside the home is explained well by Arlene Rossen Cardozo in her book *Women at Home:*

> Women's liberation has become the latest spoke in the wheel of success-ethic mythology. The women's lib proposal that a job outside home would provide a woman with freedom from boredom and loneliness at home was a treatment based on the equation of the success ethic with freedom.
>
> Men chained to specialization and sub-specialization, climbing the apocryphal ladder of success, seemed to lonely women looking out their picture windows, not enslaved, but free. Liberationists sought not to change the existing success system but merely to join it themselves. Their only quarrel with the success ethic was that it excluded women; thus, they sought to ameliorate the inequity by seeking for women the same kind of "freedom" they believed men enjoyed. . . .
>
> In theory, it appeared that a job outside the home would solve the problems faced by the woman raising a family. In fact, for many women it compounds existing problems or creates new ones.[1]

There are millions of women today who have recognized—or are in the anguishing process of recognizing—that work outside the home away from their children is not the road to freedom. They are seeing that success can be measured in the emotional luxuries a woman has as well as the material ones. This book is for those women.

But it is also for the woman I was for several years: the mother who must work for basics rather than luxuries. I made many mistakes as a working mother in looking for child care and organizing my household, but most of all, in not seeking alternative ways to work. Other women can learn from this experience. So for those women—single or married—who have no choice about working, this book is an acknowledgment of the problems and an attempt to present workable options.

I have deliberately avoided addressing the concerns of divorced fathers who have custody of their children or fathers who wish to earn their living at home in order to take a greater part in their children's upbringing. Though I initially contacted some of these fathers and found their insights wonderful, I finally felt that inclusion of their experiences would make this book unwieldy and confusing. I look forward to publications of books by these "househusbands" and "worksteaders," who, I believe, will do a better job than I could with their stories.

I should also make it clear that in spending so much time discussing women as parents, I do not mean to imply that men do not have an equal responsibility for their children. Indeed, I feel that men's greater participation today in the birth and rearing of their children is one of the most hopeful trends for families in the United States.

Most of this book focuses on women with babies or small children. This is not to say that staying home with elementary-school-aged children or teenagers is not also worthwhile. Indeed, the incidence of teenage pregnancy, drug use, suicide, and venereal diseases is assuming such alarming proportions among teenagers today that there are good reasons to stay home or work part-time outside the home during these years too. I spoke to women who had begun at-home businesses in order to be at home during the "early crucial years" and continued this work or returned to it in order to be at home during the second "crucial years." This book promotes the idea that a mother's concern for her children at any age is legitimate and laudable, rather than intellectually suspect or "self-sacrificing." The main reason for so few references to older children is principally the scope of the book as well as the conviction that things are physically and emotionally toughest on the working mother herself when her children are babies and toddlers.

In addition to being a discussion of some of the currents in our contemporary culture that propagandize against mothers' staying at home, this is also a "how-to" book. I present practical suggestions from my own experience and that of women I interviewed, as well as from research, in order to help women wishing to stay at home with their children full- or part-time. In writing this part of the book, I assumed that many readers might want to skip over one or two of these "how-to" chapters that don't pertain to their own situation, and that's fine.

I hope that this book will contribute to helping women see that there are different "seasons" in a woman's life and different solutions to the problems and challenges of each of those seasons. Career is one such season; child rearing is another. They do not always blend well. As others have said: "It's fine to 'have it all' but not all at once."

Acknowledgments

I N acknowledging the tremendous help I received in researching and writing this book, I would first like to thank the many mothers, fathers,
grandparents, and childless women contemplating motherhood who contributed their experiences, hopes, and plans. This book would not exist
without their input and support.

I would especially like to thank Cheri Loveless, Janet Dittmer, and Linda
Burton, the founders and editors of the newsletter *Welcome Home*. They and
their staff helped me with quantities of information and referrals for interviews. Just as important, they also served as models of intelligence and
restraint for my efforts to find a balance between my support of staying
home and my desire not to offend mothers who could not or did not want
to do the same.

I would like to thank Christine Compston for early criticism of the manuscript and much needed guidance on the history of women and work.
Thanks, too, to Robin Lent, Laurel Ulrich, Marilyn Power, and Janet
Polasky of the University of New Hampshire. My thanks also to the staff at
the UNH Women's Studies Library and at the Dimond Library. Special
thanks to Sherm Pridham and the staff of Portsmouth Public Library, whose
genuine interest in the book was as helpful as their assistance in research.

My cynicism about law and government quickly faded with the help given
me by congressional and senatorial aides, particularly at the offices of Representatives Pat Schroeder and Barbara Mikulski and Senators Daniel Patrick
Moynihan, William S. Cohen, and Warren B. Rudman. Thanks, too, to
Bette Jean Riordan at the law offices of Boynton and Waldron.

Though none of them could have realized what an impact their letters
would have on me at the time, I would like to acknowledge the encouragement given me in correspondence from *Newsweek* readers in March of 1982
when I expected heavy criticism for my words on working mothers and instead received praise and empathy. My thanks to my editor and others at
Lexington Books whose enthusiasm and support lit a fire under me to complete the manuscript; to Alice Boatwright for excellent editing advice; to

Carrie Sherman, Kathy Gunst, and other members of my writing group for input; to Donna Schemack, Dixie Tarbell, Marilyn Downey, Pamela Doss, and Fred and Sally Miller for their assistance and support; and to Marilyn Lima for her perceptions many years ago on feminism and mothering.

I am indebted to my neighbor and baby-sitter, Hannah Crosby, for the hours of excellent care and good times my children enjoyed with her during a long summer of research and writing.

Most of all, I would like to thank members of both sides of the family for their encouragement during the writing of this book. I am grateful to my parents for indirectly influencing the writing of this book through my upbringing: to my father for teaching me how to swing a hammer and mow the lawn, and to my mother for preferring to read rather than dust. Last and especially, I would like to thank my husband and two children who cheerfully put up with the irony of living with a woman working on a book about staying home who spent hours away from home to write it.

What's Happening Now

It is not only men's acts that disturb us—but also our reaction to them.
—Marcus Aurelius

1

Introduction:
Is This Liberation?

S IX years ago, in the midst of my Supermom days, two incidents occurred
that eventually caused me to quit full-time work. The first happened as
I was crossing the street after an appointment for a free-lance writing job I
was working on. At the time, I was putting in about forty-five hours a week
teaching two "part-time" college classes and writing and editing a report as
part of a very involved, frustrating free-lance assignment. I was worn out this
particular day, but I was also feeling like the Dress for Success Career
Woman. My husband and I were finally doing better financially after years
of after-grad-school debt. I had bought myself a striking black and brown
plaid coat and a leather satchel for carrying student papers that was, well,
sort of like a Success Symbol Briefcase. I was even remembering to wear lip
gloss and to stride across campus like Revlon's Charlie.

I was feeling impressed with how much I could take on, too. The work
days that occasionally lasted ten hours during that spring were logistical
masterpieces: scheduling children, husband, free-lance appointments, and
visits to the dentist or doctor or dry cleaner. The kids were unhappy when
their wonderful day care center closed for lack of funds, but I had managed
to get them into another place that wasn't too bad. So maybe I *could* have it
all and do it all.

That spring day I remember dashing across the street just as the light
changed and energetically leaping over the curb. I looked back to wave a
jaunty thank you to the young driver who'd waited for me to cross and
noticed that he had the most admiring look on his face. His look, roughly
translated, said: "What vitality, what energy."

I walked to the parking lot with a glow, but by the time I'd picked up the
kids, the dry cleaning, and a gallon of milk and finally got home to unwind,

I wondered how I could have looked or felt energetic. I'd been up late writing and up early to get everybody ready to go; I'd taught all morning and taken only ten minutes to eat lunch at my desk; and I'd had a long afternoon editing session with a client. As I sat on the living room couch listening to the late afternoon telecast of "Mr. Rogers" with the kids while the pork chops thawed too slowly on the kitchen counter, I felt that I hadn't been vital or energetic bounding across the street; I'd been hyper. The competency and vitality I projected at work wasn't really an act I was putting on. There simply were days when I was so revved up that adrenalin must have replaced half the blood in my body.

As the last quiet strains of Mr. Rogers' farewell song ended—my signal to start making dinner—I decided I didn't like feeling hyper, and if I couldn't stop being that way while working full-time, maybe I shouldn't work full-time.

A second incident that spring with my daughter, Jennifer, made an even stronger impression on me. On this particular "free" afternoon that I had scheduled for supermarket shopping and errands, we were driving by the children's center Jenny walked to when kindergarten let out every day at noon. As we drove up the hill, she said matter-of-factly, "This is where I always cry a little on my way to the center."

"Oh?" I tried to sound as casual as I could so that she would keep talking.

"Yes," she said, "I usually cry right at the top of the hill."

"Why is that?"

"Oh, just because I can't go home and you're not with me. I just want to go home after school."

What Jenny said hit me hard partly because she told me in such an accepting, matter-of-fact voice. She was not being manipulative. She wanted to tell me her feelings, and I'm sure she would have liked to have had things be different, but she accepted the fact that probably nothing would change.

Making Some Changes

I decided that maybe things should. I had gotten on a treadmill of working, too scared to quit. For so long, I had felt that I *had* to work; that I had absolutely no choice. But I realized that I hadn't looked for choices; I hadn't investigated alternatives. I had wound myself into an either/or bind: work full-time or not at all, live well or go into debt. But when I stepped back to look more closely, I could see that financial problems were easing for us. We had finally paid off the loan on our second car and the home improvement loan we'd taken out to put in a decent bathroom. My husband, Chip, had gotten a small raise, and although it amounted to only a few dollars a week, it coincided with the two loan payoffs.

I did a rough financial assessment of where we stood and how things were likely to go in the future. I say "rough" because I really didn't want to go into detail for fear that the exact figures would tell me I couldn't quit. It's probably just as well. I didn't know enough then to have been able to make an accurate evaluation, taking into account all the money we would save in taxes and work-related costs. I did think a lot about what I would do part-time if things got bad financially after a few months. I felt confident that I could teach at night again and kept in contact with the director of the night program at the college where I taught. But basically, my decision to quit was made on a gut level.

After I quit in the summer, we made a number of changes to save money. My husband and I sold our larger car, which was expensive to maintain, and kept our smaller one, using it on alternate days. I read books and magazine articles on economizing and talked to people over sixty who had, as young parents, apparently accepted "not having two nickles to rub together" as an expected part of having little children. After five years of seeing my son and daughter balk at the baby-sitter's door, I was ready to listen.

We did dozens of small things to save money. We learned to shut out lights, iron only five or six times a year, buy clothes at discount stores and seasonal sales, dry some of our clothes on a rack in the winter and on the outdoor line in the summer, grow produce and buy other food at a food co-op, cut our children's hair, sell our used clothing at a thrift shop, and so on and so on and so on. These are all picayune methods of saving money— but they add up and make a difference at the end of each month.

If all this sounds like work, it is. But it is work that takes up one hour a day or less, not eight. Given the choice, I prefer putting wet clothes on the drying rack to grading papers every night. I should also add that I don't feel the pressure that I did as a working mother (except for the pressure of a high electric bill) to do these things. Sometimes I'm very consistent and I'd win a gold star for conserving energy and remembering to take my coupons to the supermarket every week. And sometimes I'm not. I just try to be as conserving and resourceful as possible without feeling constrained by any one method of saving money.

In the process of writing and researching this book, I have interviewed mothers at home who have many different methods for saving and making money. One thing that stood out in those interviews was not just the specifics of buying day-old bread at a discount bakery or baking their own fresh, but the *attitude* women had. Their attitude was to hang loose, to be open to a lot of ideas, and to think up as many solutions as possible to each financial hassle.

Sometimes the answer to a dilemma is not make it, borrow it, or buy it at a discount store, but simply to do without or wait a while. Our family found that there is such a thing as an emotional luxury as well as a material luxury. For us, having me home was a luxury we wanted more than any other, and we all had to do without other things to have it.

However, we found that there are also real material needs, and careful economizing was not always enough to keep us and our household going. Seven months after I quit work, we realized that I was going to have to bring in some money. After tossing around the possibility of waitressing, modeling, or doing copywriting, I finally decided that the most comfortable thing for me to do was to teach writing again. I called the adult education director I knew and arranged a schedule. Thereafter, I taught evening classes that ran for ten weeks, and was usually assigned to alternate terms. During the "off" terms, I wrote articles and did free-lance editing, both of which I now do as a small business at home. The free-lance paychecks in combination with my husband's pay and our economizing measures are enough to get us by. When my children are only a few years away from starting college, there will be a real necessity for me to work full-time again. For now, their greatest necessity—and mine—is emotional. So I am home most of the time.

As a part-time working mother, life is now very good. But I would be wrong to wave a flag and proclaim that it is "the answer" for every working mother who is feeling overwhelmed. That would only be presenting the reverse of the idea some feminists promote: that having an outside job is "the answer" for every bored housewife. As Lee Morical points out in her book *Where's My Happy Ending?*, "The hard reality is that there are no free lunches either on the job or in the home."[1] I never liked grading papers or editing a tedious report when I was working full-time, and I'm not crazy about canning tomatoes in the heat of August, which is one of my jobs now. So there is no ideal for everyone; there is no one, all-encompassing answer to the rather knotty problem of caring for the children we love and surviving financially. A woman has to look at the options and balance those things that are most important to her and her family. It is also wise to remember that nothing is forever. Both adults and children change over the years, and therefore a woman's priorities and preferences change. The woman who loves staying at home at thirty may be itching to leave at thirty-five or forty. Or she may be compelled to go out to work because of the medical bills of an elderly parent or college tuition costs for her children.

What Are the Options?

The problem I see today is that women in my generation (thirty to forty or so) are no longer *seeing* that there may indeed *be* options. We know that our families cannot live (or live as we'd like) without our contributing, so we work full-time, sometimes barely taking a break to have babies. The result is often a complicated, exhausting situation for us as home managers, wives, and most of all, as mothers.

The response most of us give to the question "How did I get myself into this mess?" is usually "economics." But in looking back at my own life and in interviewing other women, I think the reason is more complex than that. Unless a woman is a single parent, she is often not working just to put food on the table and to pay for the electricity to eat it by.

There are basically three groups of mothers working: single parents (who are almost always broke); lower-middle-income women; and middle- and upper-middle-income women. In general, women with small children in the first two groups work because they have to, and mothers in the third work because they want to or like to have a comfortable life-style. (Obviously, this is a simplification and there is some overlapping.)

Many of us in the third group want to live well; we're used to living well. Many of the women in my generation of college graduates were raised in affluence. Our fathers were usually the principal wage earners, and whether they were teamsters or physicians, they earned enough for most of us to have quite a bit materially. In keeping with a trend that began after World War II, many of our middle-class mothers went to work when we were in high school or college, thereby ensuring more material goods and the college education itself. In our twenties, as a result of our higher education, the pill, wanting to establish a career, and wishing to enjoy the full companionship of a new marriage, many of us postponed having children.

The significance all this has for me now is that those of us who suffer conflicts about being working mothers often say, "But I *have* to work." Often this statement should be amended to, "I have to work to maintain our standard of living." It is difficult for women of my generation to do without, to lower our sights, and to recognize that there is a difference between what is *nice* to have and what is *necessary* to have.

One of the hardest things about my quitting work was that when I finally did, we had just paid off some loans and all the debts we'd incurred when my husband went back to school. We therefore had before us the prospect of living well: eating out more often, having a "real" summer vacation at a resort, getting someone in to clean several hours a week, and giving the children a lot more materially and culturally. The idea of living well was very tempting. But we decided instead to opt for an emotional luxury. It was, however—and still is—difficult to be surrounded by a society full of exciting things and opportunities and to do without most of them.

But working to live well is not the only reason so many middle-class women with small children work today. Contemporary culture communicates a message that few of us miss: it's not all right for an intelligent woman to stay home.

The women's movement of the 1960s was about women's having the freedom to make choices and to feel confident and well-adjusted, whatever those choices were. But somewhere along the line, this idea got distorted so that twenty years later there is apparently only one choice for any self-respecting, well-educated, interesting woman: to work outside the home. Current distortions of feminism dictate that this is the only place where "real work" is done. Apparently, this "real work" should continue indefinitely, even after babies are born, or maybe especially after babies are born because quickly returning to work after giving birth proves how really liberated and enlightened a woman is.

Betty Friedan told us in the 1960s that being at home with children was boring and we believed her. She is still telling people how it is and was. I heard her speak in 1982 to a large group of impressionable young college students and at first was impressed with her. Before speaking she sat on the podium looking out at the young audience, really looking, with interest and pleasure. I had never seen a renowned speaker so genuinely interested in an audience before. With her prominent nose and olive coloring she looked for all the world like an Indian chief, and I thought to myself, she *is* the chief. And then she began to speak and she lost me forever. She described what being an American woman was like before she and the modern women's movement came on the scene: "Women couldn't call themselves people. . . . There was one definition for a woman: somebody's wife or mother. . . . A woman was never a person."[2]

The friend I went to this lecture with was in her early thirties, and we both looked at each other and tried to relate Friedan's 1950s–early 1960s nonperson to our own mothers. We couldn't. In spite of the fact that both our mothers had been at home during our early childhoods and had not gone back to work until we were in junior high, we saw no resemblance to Friedan's image of the passive 1950s mother.

My Own Experience

And yet, as an ambitious and naive college student reading *The Feminine Mystique* for the first time more than twenty years ago, I accepted a lot of what Friedan said. I could see that the book was repetitive and exaggerated in places, but I needed the encouragement at the time. I was a writer just starting out who didn't have much support. It was expected by family and old friends that I would have my artistic fling after college and then get married. I would settle down when the Prince arrived. Why not? My mother had opted happily for a family and a star role in the town's Little Theater productions now and then instead of becoming an actress or designer. And after her children left home, she had had time to pursue other intellectual and creative interests.

But I was more intense and ambitious than my mother had been as a young woman. I wanted to put off marriage and family for several years and concentrate on learning to write without any distractions. And Friedan and other feminists gave me the support I needed.

In 1966, I set up house as a Young Boston Career Woman, working as a librarian days, writing evenings and weekends, and trying, trying, trying to get published. My life in Boston helped to solidify my perceptions—and prejudices—as a feminist. The main reason for that was simply the behavior of men in the city I had chosen to live in. I got tired of a good many things: being called "a girl," even when I was twenty-five and had a gray streak in my hair; seeing women friends in the publishing business who'd been Phi Beta Kappa in college making $90 a week while men who had barely made it through got $120; sitting in a restaurant feeling helpless while my date insisted on ordering dinner for me; talking to elderly male editors who assumed that most of their women editorial assistants were working to "keep busy" or for "pin money." I loved Boston and I don't think other areas of the country were much different but it was easy to get radicalized there in the 1960s.

When I got married in 1970 to the kind of "sensitive, enlightened male" I'd always wanted, I had many illusions about how things would be after we had children. In spite of my allegiance to feminism, I knew I would want to stay home with any children we had while they were babies and toddlers.

But I also felt that when it seemed right emotionally for me to work outside the home, I would, thereby sharing the financial burden of supporting a family with my husband. I even wrote a gung-ho article about this (never accepted for publication) in which I asserted that sharing the financial burden would result in fewer stress-related illnesses for men and probably a longer male life span. It did not occur to me that stress-related illnesses might simply *increase* for working women.

Having It All?

It also did not occur to me that when a woman "has it all," she has to *handle it all*. To those who still insist that we can have it all I now say, Yes, indeed, all of it: an early heart attack, midnight laundry loads, and weekend catch-up headaches. There is nothing fulfilling about fatigue. Although Friedan and other feminists writing in the sixties and seventies led us to believe that being at home with children was a consignment to boredom, they didn't remember that there are many cures for boredom, but few for the harried life of a working mother.

There is no question that many positive legislative, social, educational, and legal changes for women in the United States are a direct result of the women's liberation movement. Women now have a better chance of getting a bank loan on their own or an acceptance to law school when they qualify, instead of meeting with condescension and rejection. Women who are ambitious and commited to a particular endeavor no longer need feel that they are "unfeminine" or a "threat to a man." At the same time, many men have recognized their needs to nurture and to constructively express feelings like fear or anger. Society as a whole is benefiting, because in fields like medicine, business, and law, the best qualified of both sexes now compete rather than only men. Americans no longer assume that all little girls will grow up to be housewives any more than they believe all little boys will become farmers.

However, many of the improvements have helped those few in the upper reaches of our society rather than those in the middle, who are the majority. And, most important, there has been a tendency to "throw the baby out with the bath water." Since the 1960s we have discarded legal and social traditions that protected children as well as women. The most obvious example of this today is no-fault divorces, where a housewife and mother who may have saved thousands of dollars every year of a marriage in economizing measures or sent her husband to graduate school is awarded so little money she is usually unable to remain at home caring for her young children for even a full year. Some members of the women's movement also led male employers to believe that there is nothing to doing housework and rearing children, only to accuse them now of being "insensitive" to working women's responsibilities at home.

About the time I was thinking of quitting my full-time work, I read the words of *Toronto Star* columnist Lynda Hurst: "After the last dazzle of the [feminist] fireworks, there was deeper darkness. You are perhaps more enslaved now than you have ever been."[3] I felt as if her words had been spoken in the deep, commanding voice of an all-knowing matriarch. I began to see that women with young children and an average job—not a high-salaried executive position—were probably leading daily lives that were less liberated than that of their stay-at-home mothers. Today, many women working outside the home have less time to pursue their own interests and are no longer their own bosses as women were as housewives.

Even Jane Pauley of the "Today" show (who does have a high-salaried, glamorous position) has been affected by the reality of our situation: "The women's movement has been a boon for this generation of fathers. They get the rewards of being Daddy . . . a second income . . . they don't feel guilty and they are relieved of the stress of being the sole breadwinner in their family." In addition, with the majority of day care workers and baby-sitters being female, "the father is usually the only male the child sees. So he has no competition the way the mother might . . . the father is 'special.'"[4] To that I add that the majority of fathers also do one third or less of the housework.[5] There are many inequities.

But current attitudes interfere with the working wife and mother's seeing the absurdity of her situation. One of these involves the prevailing ideas about what a woman should do with her education. *Should* is the operative word here. As the author of *Where's My Happy Ending?* points out, "The nagging persistence of the educational 'should' can become a kind of water torture if we let it; a degree will provide us freedom of choice only if we allow it."[6]

Among the middle-class in the United States, there seem to be education-for-women fads. They range from the genteel nineteenth-century learning-to-be-ladies syndrome through the 1950s' no-better-way-to-use-your-education-than-raising-children dictum to the 1980s' use-your-education-to-get-to-the-top approach. There is no question that it is important for every modern woman to get the education or training necessary to be self-supporting. As one mother I interviewed put it, "A woman has to be prepared for death, disaster, or divorce."

But it is unfortunate when young women feel that education should be primarily connected to advancing professionally and forget that for a few years or more it can be used to help a young child discover his or her world. There is high status placed on working outside the home; we almost sanctify it. We've gone to the opposite extreme of the situation in the 1950s when motherhood was sanctified; when any woman who was married was expected to become a mother and then expected to stay home indefinitely, even when her children went off to school and she was climbing the walls. I don't think we've learned to strike a balance and to give equal value to the mother at home and the mother at work.

In the colleges where we teach the theory of infant–mother bonding in Psychology 101, we might consider discussing frankly the anguish many new mothers feel when they must leave their infants to go out to work. We might also consider instructing young women on the advantages of learning how to economize or to adapt an occupation to part-time, nighttime, or at-home work patterns when their children are young. We could discuss "early careers" and "later careers." We could acknowledge that only a fraction of working women with small children have the physical and emotional energy, the money, and the luck to blend the responsibilities of home, husband, children, and work without stress.

Conflicting Messages

Middle-class American culture gives young mothers many conflicting messages today: women should breastfeed their babies and later mash and blend "natural" foods for them instead of using that awful bottled stuff. They should hold their babies often (a tough thing to do ten miles away at the office), "involve" the father, and talk and read to their babies frequently so they will learn to be "verbally communicative" at an early age. But at the same time all this extensive nurturing is going on, a woman is supposed to be "building a life of her own" and "exploring her potential."

The media, particularly advertising, tend to exacerbate the basic problem of these conflicting messages by depicting the working woman as a glamorous symbol. She is always a "professional" on her way up, never a hairdresser or a keypunch operator or a sales clerk. She carries (always!) a leather briefcase. The briefcase, charge card, and the fast, fluid movements of the TV working woman imply that American women should hanker after the image of the male executive who's on the fast track.

Obviously, we are all free to reject this image. But like it or not, advertising is very influential, particularly when its message is buttressed by the colleges, news media, and some radical feminists.

According to a young newscaster, Lee Bergman, in creating this image of the working woman, most media people "responded to a real trend in the country, took it to an extreme, and ultimately distorted the real situation." What has happened is important because the media has tremendous power to "influence women and the society as a whole to accept the distortion."[7]

I think that this distortion had led to many problems. One of them is women's unrealistic expectations for themselves, which all sorts of dress-for-success and how-to books have encouraged. Frustration sets in when the expectations are not realized. It's not really surprising that they often aren't realized either. After all, there are only so many high-paying spots for doctors, lawyers, and business chiefs—for women *and* men. And the competition for those jobs is staggering. An M.B.A. and a subdued wool suit do not guarantee anything. A lot of us don't make it.

But in trying to make it, many intelligent, caring women are ignoring jobs that are also important and rewarding: the so-called female jobs like nursing, teaching, and secretarial work. As a result, we may, as a nation, wind up with less than qualified people in these traditionally female positions. As columnist Ellen Goodman has pointed out, what we need to do is raise the status and pay for such people instead of encouraging them out of these occupations. As it is, "the rise in status for women is associated, for better or for worse, with entry into the male world. . . . We have . . . done a better job at letting some women into 'men's' jobs *than at raising the status of 'women's' jobs.*"[8] Eventually, as shortages occur in these jobs it is possible that the salaries offered will become higher. But, in the meantime, as some of the most capable young women interested in business reject such positions, there will be shortages. This situation is no fun at all for someone trying to hire a secretary who can spell and punctuate. The business community will never be helped by a glut of M.B.A.'s and a dearth of good secretaries.

I also question whether society will be helped by women being told that it is unstimulating or unchic to be at home with their children during their early years. While the working woman is unrealistically glamorized and the single mother (or father) ignored, the married mother at home is too often depicted as a drudge; what's more, her strength in numbers is greatly minimized by the media.

For example, in the spring of 1984, a major network aired a special on women in the 1980s, that chronicled women's entry into and progress in a wide variety of occupations. But in this entire hour-long program, women of the 1980s who were mothers at home were not discussed. The field producer had in fact a great deal of footage on women who were at home, having extensively interviewed and filmed mothers who were strong advocates of staying home while their kids were young, or longer. But the footage was not included in the final editing of the special. The result was a very lopsided presentation of how American women were spending their lives. One of the women interviewed finally wrote to the producer in charge, tactfully asking why so much footage had been left out. She never received a reply.[9]

There are other instances of this type of reporting on many TV programs. On April 4, 1984, a short segment on the "CBS Evening News" reported on a congressional hearing on day care proposals that day in Washington, D.C. One of the speakers was Linda Burton, a mother at home, who suggested that one excellent way to relieve the pressure on day care facilities would be to change the dependent exemption for taxpayers so that it represented 18 percent of family median income as it did in the 1940s and 1950s. This would be a wonderful solution to the United States' child care crisis, for not only would it enable most married mothers and some single mothers who want to stay home to do so, but it also would mean less demand on overburdened day care facilities. In addition, it would enable those mothers who choose to work to pay better wages to day care workers who are now grossly underpaid.

In order for the government to be able to afford this tax reform, it has been suggested that the Pentagon and government bureaucracies would have to become more efficient and put an end to excessive cost overruns. In other words, let them pay 12¢ for an Allen wrench instead of $9,800.[10] The military-industrial complex is so powerful and so entrenched that it may be impossible to stop the overspending and use the savings to help children and families.[11] But it is an exciting possibility. This issue will be discussed further in chapter 9.

What is interesting is that when CBS reported Burton's proposal, which one congressman described as "the most appealing . . . I have heard since . . . I have been in Congress,"[12] Dan Rather's closing comment was that it was "a return to the ways of yesteryear."[13] Too often, influential media people like Rather don't seem to understand that staying at home to care for young children is most definitely involving oneself in the present—and future too—more than any other job.

Rather's remark implies not only that staying home with preschool children is old-fashioned, but also that it is unusual. Yet statistics and studies of how women spend their time do not bear this out. According to Labor

Department figures, 53.5 percent of American women with children under the age of six are employed. The 53.5 percent is, of course, a huge jump when compared to earlier statistics. But if you take a second look at the figures, you realize that if 53.5 percent are working, then 46.5 percent are not working outside the home, hardly a tiny minority. Further, if you look at how many women are working part-time as opposed to full-time, you find that 28 percent of all women workers are employed *part-time* (half days, nights, weekends, in job sharing, or in temporary jobs).[14] Many of these women are mothers of young children. If you consider that they are *at home* part-time as well as working part-time, then *over* 50 percent of the mothers of preschoolers are at home with their children *most of the day*.

One also has to remember that some women designated as full-time workers and paid full-time wages are teachers who don't work year round, nurses and waitresses on night shifts, and women who have jobs like the air-line stewardesses working the "mom shift"—a three-day-weekend shift.[15] The fastest growing group of new entrepreneurs in this country are women— people who work hard but can choose their own hours and often do some or all of their work at home.[16] Add to this the at-home child-care providers who work eight or nine hours a day baby-sitting other people's children while they also care for their own, and still more mothers at home are added to our numbers. All these facts change the picture of American mothers leaving their small children in droves, thereby creating a great social revolution. Millions of American mothers are at home with their babies and young children most of the day. *They are the majority.*

Today, the millions of American women who are lucky enough to be able to stay home to care for their young children and who find fulfillment in doing this are sometimes denigrated as women who "do nothing." They are ignored even more than single parents and given little emotional support. They are too often treated as if they were a tiny minority, not even worth considering by the media. It is time for the other side to speak up. It is time for some support and a lot of applause for mothers who choose to stay at home.

2

The Working-Mom Rat Race

W HILE the mother at home deserves attention equal to her numbers, the *real* working mom laboring both outside and inside the home does too. Notice I say *real*. We are surrounded by images of an unreal super-woman: the high-salaried attorney, the ground-breaking executive, the traveling corporate woman who takes a man out to dinner with her new credit card. The glamorous life-style of single women (well, some single women) has become muddled with that of working mothers. The general image represents such a tiny minority of women working outside the home that it has become a cruel absurdity. And yet, even when we recognize how far from reality the image is, it influences us all.

The profile of the *real* working mother is someone who may often be tired, guilty, underpaid, and stressed, even when she likes her job but especially if she doesn't. She works in an office, hospital, school, or factory. She is not very glamorous, and that's the main reason she doesn't wind up in too many perfume ads. Even in documentaries like NBC's "Women, Work, and Babies: Can America Cope?" upwardly mobile attorneys, executives, and psychotherapists are represented in a ratio of five to two to blue collar and office workers, though it is these workers who make up most of the working mothers labor force. Nearly 20 percent of working mothers are single mothers and 73 percent are married to husbands who make less than $20,000 a year.[1]

Many of us in the "real" category wound up working full-time because we put ourselves in a mortgage or life-style bind before having children and found ourselves too financially insecure to quit. Or we naively thought that it would be nothing to give birth to a cute little bundle and go back to our jobs a few weeks later. Apart from a few homemakers' magazines that many of us turned up our noses at, there is little in our culture today that encourages economizing and doing without for a few years for the sake of staying home with young children. New mothers in their late twenties and early thirties whom I interviewed also said that they had read little that even began to describe the attachment they would feel to their own small baby: "Those tiny pinhead fingernails, and the velvety hair and skin . . . the way they look up at you and reach out to you with their little hands . . ." "No one prepared me for the work and exhaustion that was involved in having a baby, but they said even less about the magic of it all."

In my own case, working outside the home kind of crept up on me. I had always assumed that I would work hard writing and teaching before having children, take off perhaps eight years to enjoy their preschool years, and then get back to work, still writing and teaching, I hoped, when I was a little old lady. That seemed sensible and, from what I'd observed, pretty realistic in the early seventies. But there were some financial surprises in store for us, especially when my husband went back to school for a graduate degree a year after our daughter was born.

We borrowed a little money from a relative and applied for veterans' educational benefits to cover tuition; my husband got a work-study job at the graduate school, and I got a job teaching writing at night to just manage living expenses. By the time my daughter was a year and a half old, I found that I could work on lesson plans and my writing during her blissfully long naps and for an hour during "Sesame Street." Since I taught and prepared classes for only fifteen hours a week, things went easily. I was very happy in all that I was doing, especially in my life as a mother.

I had had a hard time adjusting to motherhood the first few weeks, mostly because Jenny was premature. She was very frail the first two weeks after birth and could not be taken outside because of some minor damage to her lungs when she was born. I have always been susceptible to claustrophobia, but during the first couple weeks out of the hospital I wondered if a person could actually *die* of cabin fever! But once I got through the early period and Jenny began to gain weight and strength, the good times as a mother began to roll.

I found I loved taking care of a small person. Things that at first bothered me, like having milk burp-ups on the shoulder of my blouses, didn't seem particularly important after a while. I got into perspective what really mattered to me. Spending the day loving a small person seemed a pretty impressive way to live to me. I found motherhood an involving, exhausting, stimulating job.

Her first year, Jenny went out with me every day after our morning writing/nap time. On the coldest days of winter, I would wrap her in a yellow quilt and hold her close as we walked in the brittle white New England sunshine. During the spring and summer, I would put her in her orange umbrella stroller and take her for a leisurely outing downtown to window-shop and get to know the assorted dogs and cats, bubblegum machines, chain link fences, traffic cops, and other neighborhood wonders.

Jenny was a jolly, inquisitive, stubborn little kid, and we thought she was the most fascinating being that ever was. We spent a rather idyllic summer as a young family. We would eat early in the evening and then go for walks around the neighborhood. My husband would carry Jenny on his shoulders, and she would pluck blossoms from flowering trees and shower them down on us. My days with her were spent almost rhythmically as she settled into her own definite schedule of eating, playing, and sleeping, and I wove my jobs of cleaning, washing, and writing into that schedule.

During the two years that my husband was in graduate school, I continued to teach at night and occasionally had articles published in local newspapers and magazines. When he received his degree and we relocated for his new job to the seacoast area north of Boston, I was happily pregnant and excited about our move. I think I assumed that my time of working even part-time would be over for a few years. After our son, Michael, was born, I was content to enjoy him and our daughter, fix up the old house we'd bought, and write during morning and afternoon nap times. However, by the time our son was six months old, graduate school debts as well as the expenses of a house and a new baby made it clear that I would have to go back to work at least twenty hours a week.

The summer of 1977, when my daughter was three and a half and my son seven months old, I got a job in a department store evenings and, the following September, a position teaching composition at the local state university. As time went on, I worked longer and longer hours. One of the reasons this happened was the house we had bought: an eighteenth-century colonial that had originally been an eight-room home, but had been converted into a duplex during an economic depression in the 1800s. The house was about fifty yards from a cove where ducks and snowy egrets came to feed and was just down the hill from a tiny neighborhood beach.

Unfortunately, the water view and the price were the only things the house had going for it. We bought what I'm sure was the last twenty-five-thousand-dollar house in New England. Some of its more interesting drawbacks included a bedroom ceiling whose lead paint was peeling so badly that I had to vacuum it more than the floors; a bathroom toilet that was fast sinking into the cellar; and a stove with an insecurely attached oven door that would come off in your hands when you pulled it down. Our realtor had called the house a "handyman's special" with "lots of potential."

We soon learned to expect crazy experiences in every room as we slowly fixed up our "special." When we finally replaced the downstairs toilet we used a big mixing spoon to scoop up the mushy, rotted subflooring. When we took down the sagging plaster ceiling in the family room, the yellowed carcass of a small animal fell from the rafters. At neighborhood parties with friends undergoing similar experiences with old houses, our experiences now make hilariously gruesome stories.

But I have to admit that at the time it was not always so hilarious. We had to spend money and time almost every weekend fixing and patching up the place. I had to work to help support the effort. Also, we learned during the first two years of renting out half the house that we were not cut out to be a landlord and lady. In the hundred years that the house had been set up as a duplex, no owner had ever done any soundproofing. This was a big problem for us since we always seemed to rent to people who either kept late hours or had a baby who did.

So when our third tenant moved out, we decided to take over the entire eight rooms. We finally had some room to breathe and it was wonderful. But I had to keep working, and working hard, now that we had no rent money to help us make payments on the mortgage and on a home improvement loan.

In some ways, this was not difficult. I liked my job. By 1978, I was teaching composition part-time on the university's main campus, teaching the same course at night in the adult division, doing occasional free-lance editing and writing jobs, and managing to squeeze in a little time for my own writing. My job—or jobs—were fun and stimulating. And I had the freedom to work as much as I wanted each term just by teaching an extra writing course or by scouting for a free-lance job. But having this freedom made it easy for me to overextend myself, particularly since there always seemed to be some financial emergency. My last two years when I was working full-time I organized my work so that I had two half-days a week when I could be at home with my children. I would have a four-hour day, followed by a thirteen-hour day, followed by another four-hour day and a thirteen-hour day ending with an eight-hour day. I am sure this schedule every week contributed to my feeling exhausted and harried. But it was very deliberate. I wanted my children to have two half-days a week when they could invite friends over or spend time reading and playing with me.

I look back on this now as "playing 1950s mom" because so often my children were downstairs watching some dumb cartoon while I was upstairs grading papers. I would yell downstairs to pipe down or to be a big girl and get your own juice. So to a certain extent, my "quality time" with my children was a fraud. But it was an attempt at providing them a few hours a week with what I had had as a child every day: Mom at home.

On the long days, I felt guilty about being away from my children both day and night and about our inability to find a good day care situation that *lasted.* And no matter how much I might intellectualize about how stimulating my career was, I missed my children. I had a sense of "How did this happen? I never intended things to turn out quite like this." I was as maladjusted a working mother as Betty Friedan was an at-home mother. What saved me from bitterness was what saves a lot of working mothers, especially single ones: I had to work so I might as well make the best of it.

The Demands of Housework

Like most working mothers, I had no household help. In the area I live in, getting someone to clean house and do laundry one day a week costs at least forty dollars. I was a university instructor on a low pay scale. My husband was an administrator for a nonprofit agency. We had often joked about the low pay and demanding schedule we had: "doctor's hours—teacher's pay." But it was no joke that there was lots of work to be done at home and very little time for either one of us to do it.

When we were first married, we had split household work 50/50; well, maybe 60/40. Anyway, we had a small, efficient apartment to clean occasionally; three laundry loads a week; two cereal bowls, two plates, and a few glasses to wash every night; and no yard work or general house maintenance to do.

But after several years of marriage, we had a crazy, broken-down eight-room house; triple the laundry load; lots of dishes to wash; and sundry objects to pick up from any surface where a toy or bottle of juice could be dropped. And, of course, there was also the work of caring for a baby and a preschooler, which I still thought of as a demanding job in itself.

My husband spent a lot of time with the children, did the dishes most nights, cooked dinner Friday night, did his own laundry, and occasionally vacuumed on the weekends. This was all he felt he had the energy for, but it was only about a quarter of what needed to be done. I knew he needed rest at night and on the weekends as badly as he needed food and sleep to stay healthy. He left his job enervated, while I left mine refreshed at least half the time. I had much more control and freedom in my job because once I closed the door to my classroom I could do as I wished as long as the students learned what they had to by the end of each term. But in spite of understanding—and rationalizing—all this, the fact was, the unequal division of labor at home caused me a good deal of stress.

Since quitting, I've thought about the unequal division we had and that I've noticed among other married friends. I have tried to analyze why I so often did things we had originally agreed my husband would do, like vacuuming the upstairs after I had done the downstairs. He would be too tired to do it Saturday morning and too tired or busy on Saturday afternoon, and I'd finally figure, oh, what the hell, I'll do it. Now I ask myself, why did I do that? Why did he let me? I was probably just as exhausted as he was.

But I felt an *obligation* to do housework in a way that my husband did not. And I'd been conditioned to do it since I was ten. It was somehow *my job*. I think, too, that cooking and cleaning had a kind of rhythm for me that I could step to unconsciously. For my husband, it was a new dance. Why I didn't teach him how to dance, I don't know. I guess it was easier just to do it myself.

But in spite of being familiar with what had to be done, I really was not a particularly efficient housekeeper, and housework was the last thing I felt like doing. There were times when I'd finally finish cleaning on a Saturday afternoon and feel like saying, "Freeze everybody—don't eat off another plate or pull another toy or book off the shelves."

As the kids got older, things improved a little. A five-year-old can clean a room, clear and set the kitchen table, and even do some vacuuming. But beyond that, I felt that there was not much I could or should expect from my young children. So the responsibility was still mine and so was 80 percent of the work.

The thought occurred to me at the time that maybe I could just handle the frustration of dealing with a myriad of petty household chores better than my husband could. He really was not refusing to help me. He appeared to have a truly low level of tolerance as well as inexperience in attending to the daily pileup of small tasks at home. I later learned that there is some medical evidence that such a response is typical in men. Women apparently have greater tolerance for dealing with multiple tasks than men. Endocrinologically men have "a good quick response to acute stress but their hormonal make-up is not good for chronic stress. . . . Adrenalin in women is released slower and over a longer period of time. . . . Because of the difference in brain development, women can apparently deal with more things at the same time than men."[2]

However, the last thing the doctor who did this research would want is for someone to use it as an excuse for the average husband's not sharing equal responsibility for the housework. If a man has a quick, short-term hormonal response, then surely he can do household chores and errands in a quick burst of male energy. Nothing really explained why I was doing so much more than my husband; it was just a pattern that we got into.

Feeling Inadequate

At the time, I was convinced that other working mothers did not have problems keeping house to the extent that I did. The storybook success articles had influenced me so much that I really thought that other working mothers could "have it all" and "do it all."

I looked for help in different "coping books," but I found little awareness of the problems of the average, nonexecutive working woman. The books were usually written by highly paid career women. One book had a section on housecleaning and life-style that I still find a hoot. The authors discussed the pros and cons of live-in help, daily cleaning services, weekly cleaning help, and European au pair girls. It gave advice about buying more easy-living appliances, sending out the laundry as well as the dry cleaning, and being good to yourself by eating dinner out often. All sound advice for the family with a six-figure income.

The sense of inadequacy I developed extended beyond just household management to the general image I had of "the working woman." Without realizing it, I, like many women I later interviewed, became afflicted with what psychologist Lee Morical calls the syndrome of "Everybody's Got It Together Except Me."[3] TV commercials, popular books, and magazine articles and ads portrayed the working woman as one who juggled job, husband, home, and kids, smiling all the while because "I love my work so much, it's worth it."

This woman, who loved her work and her family (and most of all, herself?), seemed to be everywhere, jaunty and free, with a briefcase swinging at her side. She was an executive, a mover; she had everything under control. After all, she had a "career," not just a job like most of us. This career provided her with "real fulfillment" and gave her family a chance to buy "those little extras."

Throughout my years of working, I felt surrounded by this woman: she and her son had time to play "just one more game" before she went to work and he went to school; she dressed in cheery red and came home to a husband who sang about heating up canned soup for her; she smirked from glossy magazine ads in a full, breezy hairstyle, just the right shade of lip gloss, and a handbag, shoes, and briefcase that matched. These women, these images of success, were often in the field of business or in some previously male-dominated field. They were moving ahead—fast—and they had money.

Friends, especially male friends, who have listened to me disparage the current "selling" of the Successful Woman have asked whether this image isn't better than the old soapy one of the housewife worrying about the shine on her floor. I think the answer is that both images are unrealistic (and, by the way, we certainly haven't gotten rid of the first one). But any woman with common sense can laugh at and even feel superior to the Anxious Housewife image. The second image is discomfiting because many of us have the uneasy feeling that maybe this Competent High-Salaried Beauty is the woman we *ought* to be.

Even though she is the minority among working women, she has become important, especially among young women in their twenties. She represents a goal, the ultimate. According to psychiatrist Avodah K. Offit, many young women "long for magical, marvelous gratifications in work."[4]

The image of the woman who fulfills her dreams and succeeds in a previously male-dominated field has even invaded the women's movement. The woman who is a ground breaker, preferably on high-salaried ground, gets all the applause. Writers Richard Moore and Elizabeth Marsis have written about this in a scathing and sad commentary:

> Corporate feminism is alive and well, nurtured by enterprises that want to whitewash their sexism or simply make a buck. The bleached, coopted version of the feminist mission is increasingly passing for the real thing in the business world—and even in some segments of the women's movement.
>
> Last September, Macy's and *Working Woman* magazine co-sponsored a "special event" to unlock the secrets of success for women. . . . And though the affair promised to take "a complete look at the business of being a woman," there was scarcely a word about discrimination or harassment, sisterhood or equality. . . .
>
> By cultivating powerful but deceptive ideals of equal opportunity, business leaders hope to conceal their predominantly male hierarchies and let the steam out of calls for collective women's actions.
>
> . . . The current campaign introduces a new variation on an old theme: If women buy designer clothes and play along, they can "go places" in a man's world.

In industry after industry, women see . . . [that] the prosaic facts of their working lives conflict with the media myths about them.

Segments of the women's movement, intentionally or unwittingly, are feeding the corporate fiction that feminism is really another word for "making it." From *Working Woman* and *Ms.* to Jane Fonda and her self-help books, individual achievement and stardom are beginning to consume much of the feminist agenda. . . .

The struggles of average women, in whose name successful women are supposedly breaking barriers, have become incidental to barrier-breaking itself. Image (or tokenism, as it used to be called) has emerged as the driving force of this brand of feminism.[5]

I think that the goals of the women's movement have become quite confused in the 1980s—not that they were terribly unconfused in the seventies and late sixties. Since a lot of women don't think of themselves as part of the "feminist" or "women's lib" movement, this development would not matter except that the confusion isn't confined to the women's movement. There seems to be a growing rejection of femaleness in the push to succeed. In the media, in colleges, in the business world, "equal" seems to mean "like a man."

In an article entitled, "The Gender of Success," writer and teacher Patricia L. Dombrink explores this subject with wonderful insight:

Each year a major magazine for women devotes an entire issue to the topic of success and profiles 10 women who epitomize this concept. After diligently saving these special issues for several years and admiring the role models, I began to notice an ominous pattern. The successful women were those who had careers in heretofore male fields.

. . . The message was clear: only those women most unlike their traditional sisters are worthy of being considered successful.

Where does that leave the very successful women in the so-called service professions? Are they not successful, even when they lead happy, fulfilling lives that make a significant difference in the lives of countless other people? Have we been defining success in the wrong terms? Does the idea of success—in itself—include the requirement that a woman has broken through that previously solid barrier of prejudice that prevented her from reaching financial heights and power in such fields as engineering, architecture, law or business? Should women in traditional career fields be ignored, lest their younger sisters do something so gauche as choose a "female" career when the 1980s offer latitude unknown to their older sisters?

. . . [The] notion of aping men is . . . [also] found in the dress-for-success look widely depicted in women's magazines. The successful women are shown wearing two-piece . . . suits, tailored shirts, and carrying the obligatory attaché case. They are schooled in what to say and eat as well, in order that "feminine" characteristics do not intrude in the "male" domain of business and high finance. Prof. Henry Higgins of "My Fair Lady" would undoubtedly rejoice to find today's women "more like a man."[6]

Taking Responsibility

Though it's easy to point a finger at advertising, the news media, and various individuals, books, businesses, and organizations, women themselves must finally take responsibility for what is happening. We've unintentionally created and tolerated problems for ourselves. For all the rhetoric about sisterhood and solidarity from feminists, I fear we are growing apart, not together. For all the talk about power, in our daily lives we sometimes behave as if we were powerless.

Many of us play what I now call the macho-feminist "I-can-take-it" game. Though we may speak frankly with friends about the conflicts between home and job sometimes, we also make an effort to show people, especially bosses, that we can hang tough, we can take it. I fell into this game mostly because I was afraid some Powerful Someone (probably male and above me in the university hierarchy) would shake a finger at me and say, "See, you can't do it, sister. Go home and put another layer of wax on the kitchen floor." The words of opponents of feminism that I heard when I was a young woman in the 1960s stayed with me a long time: women are irritable and erratic once a month when they've got the curse; women job-hop; women always quit as soon as they get married. Women, in short, are not dependable or serious about their work.

In the 1960s we would counter such ill-informed criticism with statistics on women's long work records, charts of women's sick leave that did not coincide with their menstrual cycles, and other proof of women's physical soundness, loyalty and diligence. We insisted that we could be dependable and dedicated to a profession or specific job. Twenty years later, we're trying to do that; it's just that it's nearly killing us. Married women with families who work "just" part-time are in fact working full-time; those who work full-time are working at least time and a half; and single mothers working full-time are working double-time. As one writer put it, "There are, and always have been, women who can successfully cope with all the conflicts of career and family. . . . They are exceptionally hard working; they are exceptionally competent. . . . But there are, and always will be, children and women who are not so strong and resilient."[7]

The same can also be said for husbands. There is a lot of stress in two-paycheck marriages. Psychologist and family counselor Margorie Hansen Shaevitz states that working women "more frequently than they like to admit, give their partners . . . only the time that is left over—*after* the work is done, the kids' needs are met (or they are in bed), the dishes and laundry are finished, and the phone calls returned. What that usually means, of course, is that partners get the time around eleven or twelve o'clock, when the body is exhausted, the libido is quavering, and the mind is cluttered."[8]

Sometimes couples don't even see each other during the week—literally. In more than one-third of families in which both parents work, "one parent is working days while the other parent is working nights. One-tenth of these couples have no overlap at all in their work hours. . . . And 6.3 percent of the couples have only one or two hours of overlap." According to Katherine Yost, a family therapist, "this way of life is a real stresser. . . . Messages, thoughts, and feelings can get lost in the shuffle."[9]

Because wives still do at least two-thirds of the housework, some studies say as much as 89 percent,[10] there is bitterness about working time and a half. Husbands sometimes "help" with the housework or "baby-sit" the children in the evenings, but many still do not *share responsibility*, and there is a big difference. Fixing the sink or mowing the lawn once a week doesn't make up for the disparity, particularly since some "liberated" women have also taken over some of these chores. In too many families, it's chic for a woman to learn how to perform men's work but it's unchic for men to learn to do women's work.

The bitterness and general exhaustion lead to some marriages' being ruined. A woman who was a corporate executive in New York and was interviewed for a *New York Times Magazine* article on working mothers said, "I was working 60 hours a week, nursing and getting no sleep. And my husband didn't help me. When I saw how he was willing to exploit me, to let me work until I dropped, I lost faith in him and in our marriage."[11]

Not everyone has such a difficult time. The woman who doesn't have a high-level job and never brings work home with her has it much easier. But then, by media standards, she's not considered glamorous either. It is ironic that the image that has been shoved down our throats has not just been *any* working woman, but the high-salaried working woman on the fast track. Yet it is these women who must, if they are to continue to succeed, put in tremendous physical, creative, and mental energy *and time*. A woman I interviewed who had been the head of a department in a hospital said, "You simply cannot make it unless you put the time and energy into it. I worked

at home, I worked at the hospital, I worked weekends both places sometimes. To continue that with a baby and a husband who traveled extensively was impossible for me after I went back. I was afraid I would go
crazy . . . ." Not everyone with a high-level job feels that desperate. And
middle-of-the-night feedings and extreme exhaustion ease off after a few
months for any new mother. But unless she hires help, the mother on the
fast track has almost as much trouble as the single mother.

Freedom or Sacrifice?

There are, of course, women who become mothers and are unhappy or
bored at home, even after giving themselves time to adjust, and they delight
in work outside the home. If they can leave their house and children to go
out to work and everybody's happy, great. I would hate to see us return to
the rigidity and narrow expectations of the 1950s. But in an effort to replace
the detergent box or the baby bottle as the symbol of American women, we
have come up with the two-ton briefcase. Is the harried life of the business
executive really freer than the life of the housewife-mother?

Betty Friedan and other sixties feminists wrote about women spending
their lives as housewives and mothers caring for others and being lonely and
unappreciated. They considered these women self-sacrificing, denying their
own needs. But a woman working full-time in a job outside the home can
have exactly the same experience. The problem is self-sacrifice itself, and we
can experience that in the office as well as in the home. All that is necessary
is a woman willing to be sacrificed. The biggest difference is that in the old
1950s scenario, only the needs of the woman were sacrificed; now the needs
of some American children are being sacrificed as well.

3

Anxiety Attacks
at the Baby-sitter's Door

S ACRIFICE is a strong word, and in using it in the preceding chapter, I do
not mean to join the ranks of conservative child development experts
who warn of great dangers for children raised in day care. I do not believe
that early care by someone other than the parent *necessarily* results in confusion about which woman is Mom or low academic performance in school or
later inability as an adult to form close interpersonal relationships. I don't
think anyone will ever be able to devise a test that will tell us whether such
things are affected by a mother's working outside the home. There are too
many variables to consider: from the particular type of "other care" to the
individual child receiving it. But I do believe that many families are suffering
in the present child care crisis in the United States.

Social Contradictions
and the Working Woman

The historian William O'Neil once commented that society in the United
States "demands that women work, but when they do they and their children must suffer. No other developed western nation has such vicious,
irrational and self-defeating policies toward working women."[1] The problem seems to be getting worse rather than better. In a 1973 article on day
care, *Ms.* magazine used the title "The American Child Care Disgrace" and
decried President Nixon's veto of the Comprehensive Child Development
Bill of 1971. What was called a "disgrace" in 1973 is now a disaster. There
is, as of this writing, no pending bill either to help mothers to stay home in
order to care for their children themselves, or to help them find accessible,
affordable quality care while they work outside the home.

We have no nationally accepted policy of how best to care for the children of the nation. In the history of the human race, in both so-called primitive and civilized societies, this is extremely rare. There are some societies in the world in which absolutely no care is available for children outside the basic family or small social group, and there are other societies in which the only daily care for children is outside the family. But in settings that represent those two extremes, like nomadic Saudi Arabian tribes or institutionalized kibbutz nurseries in Israel, there is a prescribed way of caring for children that is understood, consistent, and agreed upon by all.[2] In this country, policymakers and citizens cannot decide whether to be for or against outside child care.

In the meantime, little has been done for mothers who feel that they must work, particularly those in the lower-middle and middle class. Women contributing to the family economically is nothing new, especially in a country like the United States, with its strong agricultural roots. But working outside the home is. After twenty years of seeing women with children under eighteen steadily, though sometimes regretfully, join the ranks of workers outside the home, we still haven't figured out how to care for children in a changed world. As a result, the average working mother with young children has a hodgepodge of possibilities for child care to choose from—or put up with.

It is ironic that in the last twenty years, women with children have in some ways lost rather than gained in status. In her excellent though disturbing book, *The Day Care Dilemma,* author Marian Blum states:

> There are long traditions of women and children being first. In fiction and in fact, particularly in times of disaster—since it was first issued as a naval order during the sinking of the *Birkenhead* in 1852—the maxim has been "women and children first." But it is an empty maxim, for women do not come first, especially when the economic realities of their lives are examined. . . . The conflicts between work and childbearing become, most often, no-win situations. Like their mothers of the 1950s, when it comes to working versus staying home, they are damned if they do and damned if they don't. Women of the fifties were caught smack in the middle of a great social and political upheaval; they had grown up expecting one set of values and common goals, and were told, in the middle of it all, that those values and goals were all wrong. If life was good, then the woman was a parasite. If life was desperate, it was because of a male, chauvinistic society. Those mothers of the 1950s who went to work early were made to feel guilty and negligent. Those who stayed home were made to feel guilty and lazy.[3]

Marian Blum goes on to say that this same problem plagues women in the 1980s so that today "women are more *last* than *first.*"⁴ It seems that in the effort to gain equality and the recognition that we were not so weak we needed a man to open the door for us, we've wound up having the door slam in our faces. Many of us were very ignorant about what was involved in having children in general and in having both children and a career in particular. Some of us have been surprised by a divorce or economic problems and find we have no choice but to combine children and a job. Whatever the situation, we are all living in a country in which the ambivalence or disapproval or confusion of those in power has resulted in no policy emerging in the last twenty years for caring for the nation's children.

I think it is important to recognize that there is a problem. Many of us pretend that there isn't, particularly to our bosses. We walk in to work, after crying in the parking lot for ten minutes, with a strong, competent-woman lift to our chins. But the fact is, leaving a child is stressful and sad and, yes, gut-wrenching. Boston writer Christina Robb chronicles some of the emotions many mothers have felt:

> For me, returning to work when my baby was 6 months old was culture shock. Suddenly there were women who smiled in compassion from behind the payroll window or the coffee urn and said, "It broke my heart, too. I did it three times." . . . At work in the last minutes I felt exhausted, as if I were pulling against some basic force of nature—and, of course, I was. . . .
>
> [Later,] after several feedings and huggings and kissings, I felt normal again, just in time to put her to bed. . . .
>
> I know . . . that to stay in touch with my daughter, I will have to feel an awful pain each time I leave her. If I stop feeling the pain, at this stage, I will stop being connected enough to her. This kind of premature separation is called for so often in American life that almost everyone I talk to who isn't actually going through the same thing tries to tell me it's not so bad. But it is. It is so bad.⁵

Christina Robb's description fit my feelings exactly—and those of other women I interviewed. One young professional woman said "The first day back, I had to pull over to the side of the road twice, I was crying so much." Though many of the women in my generation were unprepared for the depth of our attachment to our children, it is nothing new. The late Golda Meir, prime minister of Israel in the 1950s, articulated the feelings of many working women: "At work, you think of the children you've left at home. At home, you think of the work you've left unfinished. Such a struggle is unleashed within yourself. Your heart is rent."⁶

The one difference today is that, for many families, the children are not "at home"; they are at a day care center or at the home of someone else, which may or may not be satisfactory. Leaving babies and toddlers is tough, but leaving them in the care of someone we're not entirely happy with makes things ten times tougher. Although no national survey has been done that can tell us how many parents are not pleased with the care of their children, a United Way survey of parents in Los Angeles gives some indication. Only 13 percent of the working parents responding said that they had been able to get the child care of their choice. The survey was of people making over $25,000 annually, supposedly the group most able to get high-quality care.[7]

Child Care Outside the Home—
Helpful or Harmful to Children?

One of the things that is hardest on a working mother is that there is no way of knowing whether care outside the home by someone other than a close relative is harmful to children. I found that reading the opinions of child development experts and the studies done by researchers at day care centers (as well as the published discussions of the research and discussions of the discussions) did nothing to clear the mud. To illustrate, let me quote from an article in the *Los Angeles Times* that summarized some of the major studies and quoted some of the most influential experts:

> "When a child spends . . . his waking day in the care of indifferent custodians, no parent and no educator can say that the child's development is being promoted" [the late Selma H. Fraiberg, well-known child psychiatrist].
>
> . . . "Several studies indicate low morale on the part of the non-employed mother and, though it is not deliberate, an encouragement of dependency" [Lois W. Hoffman, a University of Michigan psychology professor]. . . .
>
> Still other experts . . . say their studies show that boys are likely to suffer more from a mother's absence than are their sisters, or that black children seem to thrive academically and emotionally when their mothers work but white children do not, or that the ultimate impact on the children may depend on their fathers, not their mothers.
>
> . . . Two recent studies on maternal employment and children by the U.S. Department of Education . . . concluded that:
>
> —Both elementary and secondary students living in two-parent homes perform worse on [standardized achievement] tests if their mothers work. The more hours that a woman works outside the home, the lower her children's scores will be.
>
> —The difference in test scores between the offspring of working and non-

working mothers tends to be greater for elementary school students than for secondary school students.

But the *Los Angeles Times* summary goes on to quote studies done by the National Academy of Science and published in 1982 and 1983 that

> concluded that the children of working mothers do just as well in school as the children of mothers who stay home . . . . "Parental employment in and of itself—mothers' employment or fathers' employment or both parents'—is not necessarily good or bad for children."[8]

Confusing! I could quote more from the *Times* as well as from other sources, but you get the idea. Nobody really knows how harmful—or helpful—care outside the home is for children. I doubt that there will ever be a definitive study that will tell us "how it is" for all children. For one thing, such a wide range of care exists that any one family can wind up with. Here is just a partial list:

A sister, grandmother, or close friend

An elderly neighbor

A baby-sitter registered by the state

A baby-sitter licensed by the state

An unlicensed, unregistered baby-sitter (the majority)

A nursery school with extended hours

A state subsidized community day care program

A federally subsidized day care center

A church-supported day care program

A nonprofit private day care facility

A for-profit day care center open ten hours or more

It is obvious from this list that in addition to the variety of people who can care for children, there is also a wide range of places where children are taken care of—from a brightly lit, well-equipped private or subsidized facility with an extensive playground, to a dimly lit church basement or cramped apartment.

There are also a great many individual family situations and attitudes that can affect the way children feel about going to day care. Some parents are happy about going out to work and getting out of the house—they say they are better parents for it. Some hate their jobs and resent being away from their children and home most of the day. Parents may have their individual self-esteem enhanced or harmed by their job situation. They may make a lot of money or very little.

In their personal lives, working mothers may be happily married or in the midst of grief and recovery from a divorce. They may like or dislike the sitter or day care center. All of these attitudes and life circumstances can affect children who, in turn, have their own range of feelings and experiences. An individual child may be jolly and outgoing or quiet and unusually sensitive. If there are other children being cared for, the individual child has to learn how to interact with them. They, of course, may range in personality from hypersensitive to callous. These factors alone make it clear that deciding whether or not care by someone other than the parent is good for a child can only be done on an individual basis.

Also, many of the studies done on the subject are irrelevant to the experience of the majority of working mothers because they have been conducted, almost invariably, in high-quality, university-based day care centers. Yet only 15 percent of American families use day care centers for their preschoolers, and these are certainly not all university-based, excellent facilities. Therefore, data from the studies done *"cannot be generalized to the entire world of day care."*[9]

If all of us who have worked full-time outside the home had our children in the ideal pilot-study kind of day care center (perhaps after spending their infancy at home with a grandmotherly sitter), then writing this chapter would probably be unnecessary. But most of us don't. In addition to the 15 percent who take their children to day care centers, 47 percent take their children to a sitter's home, 30 percent have a baby-sitter in the home, and 8 percent have a relative or other parent who cares for the children or the children care for themselves at home.[10] The majority of parents have their young children in an environment that is unregulated by state or federal agencies. And yet, having a child in a sitter's home or a day care center that is registered or licensed is no guarantee that the care is excellent. Few states or cities have the personnel to inspect and monitor child care facilities.[11]

The Ideal and the Reality

One can argue forever about what constitutes "excellent" child care, but there are some basics that I think most of us can agree on: safe and pleasant indoor and outdoor spaces, age-appropriate play and learning equipment, supervised interaction with other children, nutritious meals and snacks, quiet rest and reading times, and, most important, affectionate, sensitive adults who can make a commitment to caring for the children for at least a year. National research conducted also indicates that small group size is important, more significant than the ratio of adult to child. And, although the general level of education for the child care provider does not matter much, it is important for providers to have training in child development.[12]

These are really no-frill standards, the basics that all children deserve. But many working mothers will tell you that they have been unable to find such care *consistently*. This is particularly true if the parents are single, live in an area that has little care available, or are poor. Millions of women fit this description. At best, they have dependable but mediocre care; at worst, unkind or abusive care. The actual incidence of sexual or physical abuse is less than 1 percent in regulated child care centers[13] and probably is not much higher in unregulated child care facilities. Ninety-five to 98 percent of all child abuse takes place at home.[14]

The real problem with day care today is that millions of children are in mediocre, custodial care. The difficulty in these situations is not abuse but indifference. Let me give you an example. Let's say a two-year-old throws a ball several feet in a strong straight line. It is the first time he's managed that, and he's very proud. A parent or grandparent standing nearby might share in the child's excitement, acting as if this is surely the cleverest thing a little kid ever did. Obviously, such a response is very good for a child's self-esteem and self-confidence. A good child care giver might express this same kind of excitement and affectionate pride. Then again, she might not. If she is baby-sitting in her own home, a second response she might make is simply not to notice because she is so busy with her own children, the other children she cares for, and her household concerns. A third response some caretakers might make is to speak sharply at the child's cry of joy after throwing the ball so far: "Okay, so you finally threw the ball somewhere. Just watch my kitchen windows next time. And pipe down." I have heard all three kinds of responses from child care providers when a young child accomplished something new.

It is true that a mother or father could also give a response that is not positive for the child. The problem comes when the parent would give the child an enthusiastic response but has hired a care giver who would give an unenthusiastic or negative one. Then we wind up having our children raised by people who are not giving the kind of encouragement and praise we want.

Unfortunately, there are not enough of the loving, sensitive child care providers that we all wish our children could have. The following essay

describes the experience of one professional woman vainly searching for
child care:

> I missed my children when I was gone. I worried about how they were being
> dressed, fed, cared for. I worried that their bright inquisitiveness was being
> dulled by the housekeeper who, while a kind and decent person, lacked a cer-
> tain intellectual vitality.
>
> I was almost relieved when my housekeeper quit. I came back home to
> attend to my children and, again, searched for child care. Diligently, and over
> what came to be a period of two years. I searched for child care everywhere
> from the local town newspaper to the best nanny schools in London, Wales,
> and Scotland. I talked to friends. I tried to recruit at senior citizens' centers.
> Although I will admit to a prejudice against institutional day care, I even inves-
> tigated that.
>
> And I discovered that there were millions of mothers like me trying to hire
> the same sort of person I was. No matter where I . . . looked, a long waiting list
> of mothers had been there before me.
>
> All of a sudden, the notion occurred to me that perhaps the elusive, almost
> mystical "she" was not out there. After all, here we were, 17 million women
> trying to hire someone to replace ourselves. We all wanted someone warm,
> wonderful, motherly, and loving. All of a sudden common sense just told me
> that there simply weren't enough warm, wonderful, motherly, and loving
> people to go around. And even if they *were* out there, it was clear that they
> didn't want to give priority attention to *my* children. They wanted to take care
> of their own children.
>
> . . . I had wanted someone with a driver's licence, good English, a sense of
> fun, and an alert lively manner. I wanted someone who would encourage my
> children's creativity, take them on interesting outings, answer all their little
> questions, and rock them to sleep. . . .
>
> Slowly, painfully, after really thinking about what I wanted for my children
> and rewriting advertisement after advertisement, I came to the stunning realiza-
> tion that the person I was looking for was right under my nose. I had been
> desperately trying to hire me.[15]

The kinds of experiences this woman describes are not unusual for the
mother in search of the perfect "she." I knew from what I'd read and
courses I'd had in college that what I wanted was a kind, grandmotherly
woman who would care for our children in our home when they were
infants and early toddlers. When they were about three years old, this could
be supplemented with an excellent day care center or nursery school for half
the day. But I could not find anyone who was good who would come to the
house (though I did find someone who was lousy and was willing to come to

the house). I could not afford to pay minimum wage or better, and I also did not have the money to provide paid vacations or insurance or Social Security deductions. I did not have the space or inclination to have a student live with us and (again) no money for a high-priced nanny. So we did what millions of parents do: we took the children to a sitter's house.

We had several sitters over the years—what is known as "family day care." These women were, for the most part, dependable, decent people. But somehow we always seemed to get sitters who switched on the TV the way we switched on the lights when we came home. The TV was on when we dropped the kids off, when we picked them up, and the few times we called or came by early. It was always tuned to soap operas in the afternoon, which we felt had subject matter that wasn't appropriate for young children. Two of the sitters seemed to care more about having a clean house and having their day's laundry neatly folded on top of the dryer by afternoon than about playing with our children. Even in warm weather, our children and the others were rarely taken outside.

I know now that my husband and I did not work nearly hard enough to find someone we were all happy with. On the other hand, you can't be picky when there's not much to pick from. In conducting interviews, I have since realized that we were not alone in our bad luck and occasional anguish.

Some women I talked with confessed to a fantasy of living next door to an elderly woman who would take an interest in their children and love them like a grandmother. This kind, encouraging woman would become "one of the family." She would never move away.

But the reality is very different. One woman I interviewed said that she had advertised for a sitter who would have her own transportation and would come to the house, but people answering the ad always wanted the opposite arrangement. In general, she found that "the kind of person you want is the kind of person you can't get." One sitter she had forced her four-year-old to eat a hot dog he was too full to finish "till he threw up." Another sitter, an elderly widow who seemed to fit the grandmotherly fantasy, was in fact a resentful, complaining woman who didn't really seem to like the children and told them that their father was "a bad man" because he'd divorced their mother. "They were so little then they didn't understand how I contributed to the divorce, so her words really upset them. So that was the end of her."

In an effort to find a good baby sitter, many of us change sitters several times. Sometimes this creates real improvement, and sometimes it simply contributes inconsistency to the children's situation. Though I spoke to mothers who had found good, permanent care for their children, they tended to be women who were in a high-income bracket. Even those who could afford the at-home care they wanted and got it described occasional difficulties. One woman who had the space and income to hire live-in help, said, "We've had excellent women, but a *succession* of excellent women."

When a sitter isn't satisfactory and you fire her or she quits, the drawn-out process of looking for a replacement begins, and it's easy to get pessimistic about finding a person you really want to hire. You often give in and just look for *someone*, anyone, who will start right away. The fact that you can literally lose child care overnight leads to further inconsistent care and sometimes poor care. According to one child care expert, "Once you have found a care-giver, you are relieved, you think you can sit back. But child care is like a used car, once you find it, you have to keep fixing it."[16] Joan Emerson, a California counselor who helps parents find child care, found that in looking for care, "Parents tend to be desperate, and that is the basic thing that leads to low-quality care."[17]

Even when parents can find a sitter they like and their children love, there are situations that can lead to inconsistent care: the sitter can get sick for a few days, her own children can get sick, or there can be some other emergency. Some of the best sitters are professionals who may go back to school or find a much better paying job after a year or two. One single parent who had had a succession of both good and bad sitters during a twelve-year period said: "In all those years, I never had a sitter longer than a year. Even the ones who said they loved my kids had some reason for going on to something else."

The Day Care Center

Because of similar experiences, my husband and I got ourselves on a waiting list for a day care center and finally got in. Though my eighteen-month-old son had a terrible first two weeks adjusting, the center was the best experience we had. It was not affiliated with a university, but it was excellent, with energetic, affectionate young workers and a well-organized program. Because there were a number of day care teachers and a backup list of substitutes, we never had to worry about a phone call at 8:00 A.M. telling us that we were on our own for the day. This alone took a burden off us. Once the children got used to the place, it was a pleasure to take them there, and the high point of my day was picking them up and seeing them happy. But the center, one of those "high-quality facilities" a child development expert would give high marks to, closed a year and a half after we had placed our children there, due to lack of funds.

We were able to get our children into another place, although the adjustment to another school was especially difficult for my son, who was three by that time. The new place was disorganized and confused. Though it appeared to give high-quality care, it was in reality borderline unsafe simply because the supervision was so poor for my son's age group. Twice I drove into the parking area and found a three-year-old playing alone, waiting for her parents to pick her up.

Though the day care center we first had was wonderful for us, I have since learned that, apart from closing for lack of funds, centers also have many drawbacks for some parents. One problem is their institutional nature, which concerns a lot of parents who have infants or children under the age of three. This also concerns a good many child development experts and psychologists.

There is also the problem of inconsistency. The actual facility doesn't change, but the people working there do. Day care centers have the highest rate of staff turnover of any human services profession.[18] The reason for the heavy turnover is a combination of low pay, low status, and physical and emotional exhaustion—burn-out. Caring for several young children requires tremendous physical stamina, intelligence, and patience. We all have great sympathy for the woman who has sextuplets, but we forget that the experience of being a day care worker is similar. A woman (and usually day care workers are women) who is tempted to quit may try hard to stay on because she knows that the children are attached to her and that her leaving will mean one more adjustment for them. But it's logical that if this person has a degree and can get a better job, she will leave an occupation that has high demands and low status and pay, sooner or later.

Learning Independence or Growing Up Too Fast?

In spite of these drawbacks, there are some parents who will speak in glowing terms of their two-year-old's time at the day care center. They will say, "Oh, she's learning so much; she's so much further ahead intellectually than she would be if she weren't in day care," or "He's really having to learn to be independent at the center." I don't necessarily think that this is rationalization. I think parents are genuinely pleased and think that day care is good for the child. Learning independence seems to be one definite benefit to the child's being cared for away from home. I said so along with everybody else.

ı am no longer sure such "advances" are necessarily beneficial to small ᴵᵈren. Is there something inherently good in a child's learning to do things early? Some of the learning that seems to give children a boost when they enter school can be gained through an hour of "Sesame Street" every day. There is little to indicate that a child's knowing the ABCs or how to tie shoes at three will ensure that he or she will become a great government leader or an inventor at thirty. In fact, a good many of both in U.S. history have been slow learners. And, in emotional development, is early independence a guarantee of adult independence and self-confidence? No one can say yes with certainty.

A letter from a young Ohio mother raises some of these same questions:

> It seems our culture is rather obsessed with making children independent because, of course, an independent child makes life more convenient for us. [But] dependency is partly what childhood means. . . . If a child feels loved, secure, and good about himself, he will naturally, on his own time table, become independent.[19]

Each parent, of course, has to determine whether a push toward independence either in the day care situation or at home is taking place too early. But it is important not to assume blindly that early is necessarily better or that a child who appears self-reliant really is—or ought to be. Dr. David Elkind, author of *The Hurried Child*, reminds us that there is something to be said for "growing up slowly."

Children and Illness

When I look back, the incidents most distressing to me now are those that involved our not allowing our kids to be kids: scared or angry or unsure. Or ill. Illness in children is one of the things that some of the often childless "professional feminists" never talked about in espousing the notion of "having it all." Yet preschool children—*healthy* preschool children—get an incredible variety of contagious diseases like colds and the flu and chicken pox, as well as occasional ear infections and stomachaches.

When our children were sick, I felt that we ought to be ready to stay home and make them chicken soup or Jell-O. To keep them in a warm bed and stroke their heads as my mother and father had done for me. Instead, we grilled our children to see how sick they were and whether one of us really *had* to stay home. Of all the hassles I had as a working mother, this one was fraught with more conflict and guilt than any other.

A typical scene would run something like this: at 3:00 A.M., our daughter would jostle my elbow. "Mommy, Mommy, Michael is throwing up. He's throwing up so much, he woke me up." My husband and I would get out of bed to clean up Michael, change him and the bedclothes, take his temperature, give him water, rock him to sleep again, and soothe our daughter so that she could get back to sleep. We would then pile back into bed at 4:00 A.M.

An hour or two later the alarm clock would ring, and we would get up for work—maybe work. We would check Michael, trying to decide what to do. If he was hungry and fairly happy and had not thrown up by seven or eight o'clock, I would take him to the sitters or center at 8:15, praying that he would not be sick there. Out of all the times I did this with both children, there were only two times when they were so sick that we were called at work to come get them.

But I always felt guilty no matter what happened. I was guilty about taking advantage of the sitter or center and terribly guilty about leaving my kids when they were sick. If I had not been working, we most certainly would not have taken them away from a warm bed and our care when they were feeling sick and unhappy. I would also not have taken them to a place where they could expose other children to whatever they had.

But one of the reasons it happened so often was because we felt we had to save our sick leave for times when the children were really ill: when they had to be quarantined for a week with chicken pox or had strep throat or the flu. So I did not stay home with the kids when they had something we deemed minor, though sometimes the minor sniffles became major a few days later.

According to health care professionals, a recurring problem in day care centers—and no doubt in family day care too—is that parents don't always keep children home for illness, and when they do, they often bring the children back to day care before they have fully recovered. Such children then have low resistance and easily pick up infections from other ill children. It is no wonder that "day care transmission of disease is probably one of the whole nation's major health problems."[20]

But as a parent with a job, what can you do? About the only thing that works is to use sick leave for your children instead of for yourself. A nurse I interviewed said that this was so common in the hospital where she worked that she and her colleagues had an expression for it: "kid sick."

One divorced woman I talked to about illness was a junior high school administrator with a primary-school-aged daughter. One winter, the child had a severe ear infection, followed by a bout with the flu, followed by a croupy cough. The mother had no recourse but to stay home with her daughter at first, since her ex-husband lived several hundred miles away, and she could find no sitter who would care for her child. But it became more and more difficult for her to call in and say that she would be out again because her six-year-old was ill. After a couple of weeks she was lucky enough to find a friend who worked at home and was willing to look after her child while she went in to work for a few days. But later in the winter, when her daughter was sick again, she phoned the office with her hand over her nose and said that *she* was sick.

Many women feel that they simply cannot tell a boss or even some colleagues why they are out for fear that it would seriously jeopardize their job. For a single mother, telling the truth is not worth the risk, particularly if she is in the "professional feminist's" favorite occupational slot: a previously male-dominated job.

Eventually, of course, the hassles of children's getting sick lessen. Children get older and have fewer illnesses and accidents and emotional upsets and mysterious stomachaches. They can stay home by themselves when they do get sick. Children are great survivors.

Parents are great survivors too. We solve problems as they come along and try not to concentrate on the frustrations. We swap desperation stories with other working parents and learn to set up a network of friends, relatives, neighbors, and part-time sitters to help in emergencies. And some parents finally find "the perfect" child care setup.

In the course of interviewing two former day care workers, I came to recognize the mistakes we had made in looking for people to care for our children. I could see that we had not worked hard enough to find sitters whose values and priorities were the same as our family's. When we lost a sitter, we did not labor hard enough or long enough to find really good replacements. However, you have to take what you can get, and it's easy to become pessimistic. As Linda Burton points out in her essay, there simply aren't enough people out there providing excellent care. More alarming is the fact that in this country, some parents who must work to stay off welfare cannot find *any permanent care at all.*[21] So a child of four or five is shuffled from temporary sitter to neighbor to friend to, occasionally, the back seat of the mother's car or left in an empty house.

There are various policy changes and concrete improvements that could be made on federal and state levels that I will discuss in chapter 9. But as it is, federal subsidies for child care have been reduced for low-income parents.

There is no help for middle- and lower-middle-income groups, apart from some private and community referral groups in some states and a few corporate on-site child care facilities. Women who work sometimes make so little money after paying day care expenses that it is only the unpleasant alternative of welfare that keeps them going. Yet middle-income married women who want to stay home have difficulty doing so economically. Divorced women who might be able to afford to work half-time or during school hours often can't because the courts do not consistently prosecute ex-husbands for reneging on child support. Among these men are orthodontists and successful businessmen.

Those of us concerned about all of this are left with many questions. I fluctuate between feeling that maybe children with mothers at home in the 1950s and earlier were indulged, to feeling that children are vulnerable, needy, powerless beings who cannot adequately articulate their wants and needs. I ask myself whether the rough-and-tumble of a day care center is good for little children. Or do they need, when they are tiny, as much protection and holding and individual attention as they can get? Does growing up with a group of children help children learn to interact with their peers? Or simply cause them to be overly aggressive or susceptible to peer pressure? Do the disappointments children feel when nobody can leave work to drive them to an after-school birthday party, or to see them in a school play, make them tough and resilient? Or simply insecure? In short, when we accept, even promote, a childhood for the nation's children that is less secure and nurturing and consistent than what many of us benefited from, are we being rational—or simply rationalizing? Is anyone being liberated?

II

Making Some Changes

What you have may seem small; you desire so much more. See children thrusting their hands into a narrow necked jar, striving to pull out the sweets. If they fill the hand, they cannot pull it out. . . . When they let go a few, they can draw out the rest.

           —Epictetus

Making Some Changes

4

Can You Really *Afford* to Quit?

B Y the time I quit I felt that I would rather eat spaghetti every night than keep us all in the working-mom rat race. I simply didn't care about the money. When I quit in the summer I figured—pretty vaguely—that if things got bad financially by September, I could probably get a teaching job at night for a few hours a week. Once you've gotten to the point where you are *ready* to quit full-time work and stay home with a child or children, it's tempting to quit on the spot. But I don't recommend it.

I once worked with a woman who had a mini–nervous breakdown as a result of late night feedings, indifferent sitters for her baby, and the irascible, demanding boss we all shared. When she walked out one evening in the middle of unfinished work, the last thing she said was, "This'll fix the boss, that creep." While this was a fitting description of our boss, walking out did not "fix" her; it did a number on the rest of us. We had to cover for this young mother and deal with an employer who was more temperamental and nasty than ever.

So, no matter how stressful the home–work situation is, it's best to quit after at least a little forethought and two weeks' notice. This isn't just courtesy and kindness talking, it's practicality too. You never know how many years it will be before you want or need to go back to full-time work, and sometimes an old job is the first and best place to look.

I also think it makes life easier for everybody in the family if some preparations have been made ahead of time. Sitting down with paper and pencil and making some evaluations of your finances, emotions, and community is wise. And if the financial assessment looks grim for you as a one-paycheck family, then it helps also to look at the possibilities for part-time or at-home employment.

Making a Financial Assessment

The best assessment to do first is definitely the financial one. This is just a cousin of the monthly budget most of us are already familiar with. If you have never done a budget, Sylvia Porter's *Money Book* is a good reference. There are also thin booklets you can buy at a stationer's shop or a dime store that are written specifically for this. When listing your present expenses, keep in mind that it's crucial that you remember *all* expenses.

According to financial experts, when people review their finances, they're often worried that they will only learn what they can't do. But, according to financial experts, planning gives you "greater control and well-being." Parents who want to have the mother stay home have to change their financial priorities and "recognize the need for trade-offs."[1]

Once you have a basic budget for the average amount you spend on items each month, take a close look at the individual items and begin putting values on things: what you *need* and what you *like*. On two separate sheets of paper, transfer budget items to a "Need" List and a "Like" List. A working couple with one child might wind up with something like tables 4–1 and 4–2.

When both lists are complete—and it usually takes a week or two to think of *everything*—type or print the lists and get at least two photocopies of each list. That way, you can play around with scratching out and reentering items without totally obliterating the lists.

Table 4–1
"Need" List

	Cost
Monthly bills paid on time:	
Mortgage	
Utilities	
Gas	
Electric	
Water/Sewer	
Fuel	
Installment payments:	
Car loan	
Refrigerator loan	
Master Charge bill	
Insurance premiums	

Bills coming in twice a year or more:

Medical and dental bills

Maintenance costs on house and yard

Taxes:
  Property
  Residence
  State
  Federal

Dues for professional organizations

Clothing:

Work

Recreation and home

Children's

Transportation costs, maintenance on car(s)

Personal grooming:

Haircuts

Cosmetics

Other

Furniture for children and house

Food:

Groceries

Snacks and coffee breaks

Lunch out at work

Savings

Unexpected expenses

Entertainment (leave blank until Like List is completed; alter after doing emotional evaluation)

Table 4–2
"Like" List

	Cost

Entertainment:

Weekend movie twice a month

Dinner out once a week

Lunch out on weekend

Other treats:_____

Concerts

Party with friends occasionally

Raquetball one night a week

Travel:

Occasional weekend trips

Summer vacation

Long winter weekend away

Lessons and classes:

Art

Music

Aerobics

Books and records or tapes

Children's books and toys

Charitable contributions

Gifts

Extras:

Full liquor cabinet

Other: _____

As you've probably guessed, the purpose of these two lists is to figure out what you can comfortably cut out of your Like List and cut down on in your Need List. The key to doing both successfully is to find a lower-priced replacement for an item, rather than dropping it entirely. Cutting out the basic things on the Need List is impossible, and removing everything from the Like List can lead to problems: resentment on the part of the person working outside the home, and a feeling of being "stuck" or "poor" for the person at home. So avoid being savage.

Reducing Expenses—The "Need" List

Though it may seem that the most you can hope to do in order to economize is take things off the Like List only, you can usually change more things on the Need List than you'd expect.

Buying a House. If you are thinking about a major purchase, like a house, think again. More young mothers get caught on a treadmill of working because of high monthly mortgage payments than because of anything else. Sometimes there is no way of avoiding this. As one young woman said, "If you want to have children you don't want to raise them in an apartment, and sometimes renting a house is almost as expensive as making monthly mortgage payments." However, if you are thinking of buying a house, but haven't yet, consider all the alternatives carefully: a smaller house, a less expensive neighborhood, a duplex or house with a small apartment you can rent for income, building a small, basic house and acting as your own contractor, or a house in need of cosmetic improvements you can do yourself. High mortgage payments are the number one nemesis of stay-at-home mothers, so consider a home purchase carefully or wait a few years.

Utility Costs. These costs can be reduced in several ways. For specific help, contact the utility companies themselves, read state and federal pamphlets on energy saving at the local public library, as well as magazines or books relevant to the subject that you see at the library.

If, like our hypothetical working couple with one child, you have loan payments, check to see how far along you are in paying off the loans. You might want to pay off a loan before quitting, reduce it, or sell a second car so you don't have an item like "car loan payment" on your Need List at all.

Medical Expenses. No one can do without medical attention for a serious illness or injury, but you can read up on what symptoms indicate a severe ear infection in a child or simply a mild cold that a parent can treat without paying to be told how. I have spoken to a couple of women who have found good, sensible books on home medical treatment. Some of the books out today are what my husband calls "hippie quack books," but others are dependable and written with sound medical advisors. In fact, one of Dr. Spock's original purposes in writing his famous baby book was to assist parents who did not live within easy access of a doctor.

Attending to some medical needs yourself is, according to futurist Alvin Toffler, a growing trend:

> Today mothers are taking throat cultures. Schools offer courses on everything from foot care to "instant pediatrics." . . . Sales of otoscopes, ear-cleaning devices, nose and throat irrigators . . . are all booming, as individuals take on more responsibility for their own health, reduce the number of visits to the doctor, and cut short their hospital stays.[2]

Preparing chicken soup and offering a cool hand for a feverish forehead is, by the way, in the best tradition of a mother at home. So, using care, try to determine what savings are possible for you in health care. Look into Health Maintenance Organizations, community clinics, and other alternatives.

Home Maintenance Costs. Moving on down the list, maintenance costs on a house can be greatly reduced by doing as much as possible yourself. Again, there are lots of books and other resources to help here. One of the most significant savings in maintenance I made my first year at home were in repairs I did myself that were crying to be made: replastering small holes in the walls in the hallway, applying roofing cement to a low roof that leaked, and caulking around the windows outside. I knew nothing about these things and regarded the replastering job with great trepidation. But an un-expected bonus in muddling my way into these tasks was that I learned some new skills and had a boost to my morale as a woman who did not have to rely on hiring a man to do such jobs.

Taxes. If only they and death *could* be avoided. But, according to writer and new father, Peter Spotts, whose wife stays home with their baby, this item on the list can be tamed. By changing the allowable exemptions on federal W-2 forms and state income tax forms at the father's workplace, your one paycheck can yield additional money for monthly expenses. In his home state of Massachusetts, making this change gave Peter Spotts's family a total of $140 a month.[3] Many mothers who quit say that at tax time their family's lower tax bracket means significant savings for them.

Buying Clothes. These mothers also cite substantial savings in clothing when they quit. Clothes for work usually cost more than those worn around the house. And at-home mothers have time to shop for sales, to find good discount stores, and to get kids' clothing at thrift shops. So figure on a reduction in clothes, even if you're not planning on doing any sewing. How to save money buying clothes is discussed in detail in chapter 5, "Saving Money instead of Making It."

Food Costs. Increases in food costs in the last decade have meant that this budget item on the list takes a much bigger percentage of our monthly incomes than it used to. But it's possible to get around this problem by growing some of your own food, joining food co-ops, buying in bulk, and using supermarket savings gimmicks, as described in chapter 5.

The Importance of Savings. Sylvia Porter and other economists insist that you set aside money for savings and unexpected expenses no matter how small your income. Even if the amount saved is only five dollars a week, you should still set this money aside. Some at-home mothers earmark about 60 percent of all the Christmas and other gift checks that come into the family for savings when they don't have any surplus after budgeting basic expenses.

Adding Up Income You May Not Have Thought Of. If you are like we were, your Need List total expenditures may add up to an amount that's close to that of the one paycheck you have to live on. But don't be discouraged. One other step is important in determining exactly where you will stand financially: add up the money you will have coming in apart from the one paycheck, like bonuses, interest on savings or NOW accounts, gift checks from relatives, likely tax refunds, the sale of a car or extra TV, and so on. Think of all this as money in the till, money to live on—because it will be.

Also, if you have never taken deductions on your federal income tax forms or have hired an accountant to do your taxes, consider spending several hours learning to do your own taxes in the spring. Until the U.S. tax system is changed, you can take deductions and credits for donations to your church or synagogue, home mortgages, some local taxes, and interest on loans, to name a few items. It takes me at least a full day to do the forms each year, but we get IRS refunds of $90 or more and save another $50 by not hiring an accountant to do our taxes. For a day's work, $140 is not bad pay.

Reducing Expenses—The "Like" List

When you've done all you can to determine your new income and your essential needs, look at the Like List. Knock out, cut down, or find inexpensive substitutes for as many items as you can. In doing so, remember that this is not forever. There will be a day when your children are older, and you'll have two paychecks again and can put all the items back on the list.

How to Make Money-saving Changes. Let's say you have "aerobics class at health club" one night a week on your Like List. In finding an alternative, you might consider whether it could be replaced with a one dollar a week kinder-gym class with your child at a local community center. Or you might decide simply to walk or ride a bike more. One woman I interviewed said that she was able to keep her weight down consistently (and also get "time away alone") by taking long walks in the evening while her husband got the children ready for bed.

A week's summer vacation at a four hundred dollar a week cottage could be replaced by a week in a national park's cabin or a visit with an old college friend and her family, which would later be reciprocated. On some U.S. and Canadian college campuses, it's possible to stay for a week or more in a college dormitory during the summer for a half or third of what it would cost to stay in a nearby motel.

"Likes" That Are "Needs." Once you have performed surgery on your Like List, it's important to put the items you can't bear to strike out onto your Need List; then toss out the Like List (you might as well get used to doing without the extraneous). It may seem odd to add these items to the Need List, but if you have had trouble crossing off an item or finding a replacement, it is probably because it really matters to your family, so it *is* a need—emotionally.

I cannot stress enough how important it is to include important Likes on the Need List. The more rest and relaxation you have, the easier it is to drop *things* from the Need List: a new piece of furniture, a new car, a large wardrobe, and so forth. The idea is to attend to the basic, physical needs you have without going into debt and get the same *or more* recreation and relaxation. The purpose of the financial assessment is not to consign families to a sterile, static life-style, but to determine what they really need in order to remain physically and emotionally healthy as individuals and as a family.

Making an Emotional Assessment

That brings me to the next evaluation that needs to be made: an emotional or psychological assessment. This involves an honest questioning of whether everyone in the family can eliminate things from the Like List, find alternatives, and shift priorities. In short, can everyone handle doing without for a few years? This question follows logically from the financial assessment because in making that assessment first, what is really important to whom comes out pretty dramatically. And the fact that there is going to be a lot less money becomes obvious. Assessing your ability to live in slightly (or greatly) reduced circumstances is more important to your success than determining how much you'll save on transportation costs or how many discount stores are located near your home.

Individual Needs. There are some people who, in honestly questioning themselves, may decide they cannot do without. For example, a woman who was the youngest of several children and the recipient of large numbers of hand-me-downs and at thirty is a compulsive clothes buyer might be such a person. However, continuing to work is not necessarily the answer. There might be several other solutions to this problem, from professional counseling sessions to learning how to sew clothes instead of buying them. But it is crucial to acknowledge a partner's difficulty in doing without because one of the great things about a mother's quitting her job is what good things it can do for her marriage. Such things won't happen if one partner has a lot of resentment or insecurity about the family's reduced income.

One woman I spoke to was married to a man who was insecure about money in spite of his relatively high salary and the hefty sum they had been able to save before their baby was born. He was upset that his wife insisted on quitting her job permanently. Ironically, they eventually saved more money each month when she was at home because she changed her clothing- and food-buying habits. But whether she saved money in a given month or broke even, she put everything down on paper to reassure him that things were okay, that they were going to make it.

As the characters of cartoonist Berke Breathed remind us, we all have a "closet of anxieties." Sharing the financial responsibility of raising a family has been one of the bonuses of the women's movement for men, and taking this bonus away in part or completely can be very unsettling. As one husband said, "This feels a little like launching a rowboat with only one oar." It's important to keep lines of communication open and, especially the first few months after quitting, to keep a constant eye on how well funds are holding out.

In evaluating your psychological and emotional attitudes, avoid "shoulds" and "should nots"—toward yourself as well as toward your partner. For example, "I shouldn't care so much about replacing the ratty living room couch with a new one; staying home with my three-year-old should be enough." If getting a decent-looking couch is important to you, it's important. So, before quitting, have it recovered, buy a new one, or get one later at a yard sale. Avoid expending psychic energy telling yourself how you "should" be feeling.

Social Pressures and Isolation. In addition to dealing with personal hang-ups and fears about finances, it is also helpful to look at your family's social life and immediate community for any pressures that may be there. What are the social expectations? Are you living in an upper-middle-class community where children go to private kindergarten at five and have a ten-speed bike by the time they're nine? Do you belong to a social or athletic club where people think little of dropping fifty dollars on a Friday evening?

In our own case, my husband and I had never gotten into this kind of social milieu, and we live in a neighborhood that is pleasant but hardly chic. Because I quit when they were three and six, my children became accustomed from an early age to doing without, "buying used," or setting aside allowance money for various things. But in some areas, particularly in suburbs of large cities, there is a lot of pressure to consume and compete. In such areas, it's tough for the kids of a stay-at-home mother to keep their feet on the ground in their factory-second sneakers. It's well to keep all this in mind if you're in the market for a house; you want to be sure you're living in a neighborhood where your values won't be out of place.

In making a family evaluation of feelings, you should also think about the disadvantages of staying home; the isolation and loneliness a woman can feel initially—or sometimes longer. This usually is not a problem once you meet other women who are at home, and there *are* millions of us out here. But having both a husband and wife identify disadvantages to staying home can sometimes lead to surprising results if both earn roughly the same salary. I know of two situations in which the wife's salary was enough to support the family, so the husband stayed home with the children while she got out of the house. In one case the husband did part-time consulting when the children became of school age, and in the other the father was content to involve himself in rearing the children for several years.

However, from the interviews and research I did, it seemed that mothers found leaving young children more "gut wrenching" than did fathers. For that and various other reasons, it is usually still the mother who wishes to stay home. But it is important to be flexible and open to the possibility that in some cases it is better for the father to stay home.

Whoever winds up at home, it is wise to create a short transitional period before you quit your job, during which you try out living on one paycheck. Although this transition may be a little misleading financially because you don't save on commuting and other work-related expenses, it is still helpful. It enables you to see what it's like to live modestly, with lost-cost alternatives for both basic and emotional needs.

Assessing Your Community

Once family members get clear on everybody's feelings about living on a reduced income, it's important to take a look at the area where you live, analyzing how it can help you to economize and also enjoy life in spite of your having a reduced income. Are there brand-name outlet stores in your town where you can buy clothes and shoes? Thrift shops where you can buy and sell children's clothing? A dairy farm, bread factory, or day-old bakery outlet where you can get inexpensive milk and bread? Is there an open produce market, meat market, dockside fish market in your city? Are large, individual garden plots on town land available to residents in your community? Is there a food or baby-sitting co-op in your area? Finding the answers to these questions can make for some interesting "field trips" for your children and can enable you to see how much you can save in your own neighborhood.

Living in a Wealthy Area. If you live in a wealthy urban or suburban area, where most residents have little interest in economizing, this whole process may seem a bit discouraging. But over time, you will become aware of things that will provide savings. And if you do quit working full-time, you will meet an incredible number of people in the same boat through your children. (Who is sitting under the trees at the park while you're hunched over your desk each day? At-home mothers who are broke. They will be willing to reveal their secrets.)

"Cheap Thrills." In analyzing how your community can be a source of savings, take note of what is available purely for recreation—"cheap thrills,"

as one couple put it. Check out the parks, public tennis courts and swimming pools, local "Ys" and community centers, state colleges, churches, synagogues, and public libraries. Even places that charge admission, like museums and botanical gardens, may have low or free admission during certain hours or seasons. Theater tickets are free in some regional theaters if you usher or provide some other service. Movies usually cost less at matinees, and drive-in movie theaters aren't too costly when you consider that you can take the children with you to some movies and save on hiring a baby-sitter. There is probably a great deal more available than you realize, especially if you live in or near a city with a population of more than twenty-five thousand people.

Living in the Country. If you live far from a city or town, then it's likely that you're in a rural, physically beautiful area. There's a lot to be said for swinging on the bough of an old beech tree. In the country, a stay-at-home parent has a special opportunity to revive practices like maple sugaring, raising animals that produce dairy products, or heating with wood—practices that save money and give children good skills and experiences, as well as provide family enjoyment. There are advantages and disadvantages to any location that a family might live in; the parent at home needs to concentrate on the advantages and make the most of them.

Alternative Employment

After looking at finances, individual feelings, and community advantages, you may feel that your family cannot get along happily with only one paycheck. At this point a woman committed to staying at home can delay quitting her job for several months, saving at least half of every paycheck so that she can later afford to stay home. This approach, however, can be a little risky. As a four-year practitioner, I finally dubbed this the "Mañana Syndrome." It can go on indefinitely.

It is sometimes better to assess what opportunities are available for what I call "alternative employment": part-time, evening, temporary, half-day, short-term, or at-home work. There are growing opportunities for this kind of employment today. One out of every five jobs in the United States is part-time, and more of these positions are opening up every day. According to the Work in America Institute, by 1990 about half of the jobs available will be part-time.[4] Though part-time jobs have traditionally been low-paying and nonprofessional, this is beginning to change, especially in flex-time and job-sharing situations.

One of the first places to look for a part-time job is at your present job, assuming that one of the reasons you want to quit isn't your dislike for your present occupation. Women I have interviewed who have transferred from full-time to part-time hours have said that a job that was overwhelming five days a week became wonderful three full days a week or five half-days.

There are also weekend and evening jobs, though they may not pay well. However, if what you care about most is fitting paying work comfortably into your life as a mother, they are sometimes the best jobs to get, especially if you only want one for a few years. Sometimes, they also lead to friendships with other mothers who have similar needs and priorities.

Although it is unusual for a woman to survive financially with part-time work if she is divorced, unmarried, or widowed, it has been done. It helps if you have only one or two children and some savings, as well as a network of emotionally supporting relatives or friends. A single mother with a baby son described trying to find "the right balance between earning an income and being at home" and wound up doing day care in her apartment in the mornings, teaching at night a few hours, and occasionally offering parenting workshops. "All of these jobs combined don't take me away from [my son] as much as one office job would, and I'm free to rearrange my schedule." As she herself admitted, not all single parents have "her particular set of skills or . . . drive." Nonetheless, she thought that for most women there are "alternatives if they want to stay home with their children."[5]

The alternative for many women, both single and married, is to set up a modest business at home. For someone with a lot of energy and organizational skill, doing this offers a challenge and can sometimes turn into a larger, more lucrative business when children in the family get older. In deciding what specifically to do, it's best to consider your community's needs and then write down your education, experience, and interests. As many at-home businesses have developed from a woman's hobby as from her original full-time occupation. (For more information on part-time work both inside and outside the home, see chapters 7 and 8 and appendixes A and B at the end of the book.)

Enjoy Being at Home!

Recently, some excellent magazine articles and paperback books have been published on how to set up a business at home. Unfortunately, some of the how-to information gives the impression that if a woman doesn't work for pay outside the home, she's got to work for pay inside the home, which simply contributes to the Superwoman Syndrome. If you are thinking of quitting, and it isn't immediately necessary to bring in some money, then don't—just enjoy being at home. Often, even with a financial assessment, a couple can't tell how well they will eventually manage to do without the second paycheck. So it's best to wait a while before plunging into a part-time job or at-home business. In the meantime, consider that running a home and raising small children is a more than sufficient occupation.

5

Saving Money
Instead of Making It

ALTHOUGH I did not know enough at the time I quit my job to make a formal assessment of our family finances, I knew that we would have to make a great many changes in our lives in order to stay solvent on one paycheck. I was going to have to figure out ways to save money, since I wouldn't be making any for awhile. My children were three and six, old enough not to need constant attention, so I figured that one thing I would have would be time, which I could use to economize. Many of the changes we made as a family and incorporated into our daily lives were picayune and were, by themselves, inconsequential. But coupled with some major changes, they made a big difference. They added up at the end of the month, and, maybe more important, they reflected a change in attitude: we became more questioning, self-aware, and resourceful.

In making individual changes, flexibility—bordering on off-the-wall looseness—was a big help. I found some unusual ways to save money. My family's favorite was the time my daughter had outgrown her ballet slippers two weeks before her spring recital and last lesson. In the past we had decided that it was okay for the slippers to be snug by the end of the school year so that we wouldn't have to buy another pair. When my daughter outgrew the slippers early that spring, I was not about to buy a new pair and have them sit in her closet all summer after being worn twice. So I lathered saddle soap onto the slippers to soften them and then stretched and pulled gently at the leather in the toes to make more room. Then I hung the slippers from hooks on the bathroom door and weighted them down with smooth stones from the beach to stretch them some more. Two days later, the slippers fit perfectly.

My daughter thought her mother was "very strange" and did not want me to tell anyone about the way we had managed to avoid buying new slippers. But two years later, at age eleven when she was growing so fast that we had to buy a pair of slippers twice during the year (and even then the second pair was snug by April), she asked me for instructions on how to stretch her slippers. A few hours later I found the soft pink slippers swinging on the bathroom hooks stuffed with small stones.

Sources of Information on Saving

Though we invented many of our own methods for saving, we also borrowed from some excellent sources. One of the best sources was a book entitled *The Heart Has Its Own Reasons*, which describes a wide range of ways to save, from major considerations like housing to minor ones like using rags or newspapers for cleaning instead of paper towels. I found that the public library and the paperback section of the local bookstores were invaluable for finding the help that I needed. If you want a book but it's too expensive to buy, ask your librarian to order it for you. Many people forget that most public libraries have what is called an "acquisition budget." Librarians like to know what books their "customers" want, so don't ever hesitate to ask for a specific book or periodical. There are books on budgeting with money-saving tips that I have taken out of our library three and four times. If a book has several pages that I find very useful, I will photocopy them. Even a dollar in coins fed into the photocopying machine is less than what you would pay for most softcover books.

During my first six months at home, I read various pamphlets on saving energy and articles in women's magazines at the library on food management. I had always looked down my nose at how-to-stretch-your-food-dollar kinds of articles when I was working. I didn't have the time or patience or energy to try their recommendations. But I set aside my skepticism and began reading such material carefully. I also sent away for information and attended two free workshops on energy saving given by our state university's cooperative extension service.

On a different note, I also reread Peg Bracken's book, *I Hate to Keep House*, which I had received years before as a wedding present from some discerning true friend. When I stopped working, I had mistakenly assumed that I would miraculously turn into a wonderful housekeeper just because I was at home. We were all sorely disappointed in this. In fact, with three of us at home all the time, the house had the potential of getting into a bigger mess than ever. But *I Hate to Keep House* helped me to keep a sense of humor and to realize that I could do only so much. Besides, my shocking deficiencies as a housekeeper saved us money—the less I vacuumed the house, the more electricity we saved. The more I served carrot and celery sticks for the vegetable at dinner instead of chopping and cooking them, the more gas we saved.

Peg Bracken's book, *Hints from Heloise,* and *Mary Ellen's Helpful Hints* were all a help. The materials I read encouraged me in my hope that time could be our edge against inflation instead of a second paycheck. So I urge anyone who is quitting full-time work or thinking of doing so to check out all the resources available. There is lots of help out there.

Specific Ways to Save Money

From such resources I gleaned dozens of ways to save money. Here are a few, with some contributions from several other families, just on clothing and personal appearance items:

Buy children's clothing at regular store sales and factory outlet stores, or at dependable thrift shops.

Sell all clothing you're not wearing to thrift shops or have a yard sale; what you don't sell, give to charity, estimating the fair market value and taking it as a charitable deduction on your income tax.

Dry clothes on the clothesline outside; inside, on a drying rack.

Iron only a few times a year; when you do iron, do a lot all at once.

Spot-clean or brush woolens whenever possible; air dry wool suits to keep them fresh.

Wash knitted woolens in cold water and mild liquid soap.

If you have the talent, make clothing, tote bags, bedspreads, curtains, and other things, preferably using sale fabrics and remnants.

Cut hair at home or go to a barber rather than to a hair-dresser; consider having Mom's hair shoulder length so that frequent cuttings are not necessary.

Ask for expensive perfumes, makeup, and after-shave lotions for Christmas or birthday presents when relatives ask what to get.

"Cherry pick" for soaps and shampoos (check out prices any time you're at a supermarket, dime store, or drug or beauty outlet store, and stock up at the place that sells a good brand for the least amount).

Store soap out of the wrapper to minimize its gooiness when it's wet, thereby lengthening its "life." The stored soap also perfumes drawers.

Buy dress shoes and other shoes you don't wear frequently that are made out of high-quality vinyl. Save your money for leather boots and shoes you wear every day.

Buy high-quality underwear, but try to buy only at sales.

Buy supermarket stockings and stick them in the freezer for a day to lengthen their life.

Buy a minimum of all clothing and in fabrics that are long-lasting.

Color coordinate clothing for both children and adults so that everything goes together and nothing is "wasted."

If you have a baby, use cloth diapers instead of disposables.

Let your children wear minimal clothing in the summer, like shorts and no shirt. Get them in the habit of wearing layers of clothing in the winter inside the house.

The list could go on and on. The point is, you can revive and invent all kinds of saving methods once you start thinking about what life was like before paper towels.

I will be the first to admit that some of the economies are a pain in the neck. As a result, I, as well as many other at-home mothers, do not stick rigidly to all our methods of saving at all times. Often you can stop saving in one particular area where it no longer seems "worth it," and rigorously, consistently save in another area.

Saving Money on Clothes. Sometimes children dictate changes. It's wise to take advantage of the fact that while your children are young, they don't know the difference between brands or care. For example, babies do not know when they are wearing secondhand clothing. Three- or four-year-olds are more aware, but if clothing comes from an admired older neighbor or cousin, their secondhand clothes can actually be a source of pride. School-aged children are sometimes bothered if all their clothes come from a thrift shop or a neighbor child. Older children care a lot. But in that case, you can buy at good outlets, ask for clothes from grandparents for birthdays, and also let children buy some items with an allowance or earned money. If free or inexpensive clothes are a source of delight rather than embarrassment for you, it's likely that they will be for your children too. Mary Ann Cahill, author of *The Heart Has Its Own Reasons*, reminds us that "it can be said unequivocally that there is no evidence that a child suffers any mental or physical trauma from wearing secondhand or handmade clothes; the same cannot be said when substitutes are made for mother-at-home."[1]

Saving Money on Housing. Babies and little children are also quite unaware of how large or well decorated their houses or apartments are. So the home itself can be a place where you can make major savings. As I said in chapter 4, high housing costs can be a real nemesis of mothers-at-home. In responding to this fact, it's important, once again, to be very flexible. If you have not yet bought a house, can you wait? Or can you buy a smaller house? An older home? A duplex with another couple? Or could you be happy buying a large house that has separate living quarters for a tenant or an elderly, rent-paying relative? Do you have the interest and background to act as a "house parent" in a halfway house or home for retarded adults? Could you buy a nice house in an inexpensive neighborhood that's "coming up?" Do you have the minimal skills and patience needed to fix up a solid but neglected older home? Or to build a small house with plans from Acorn Structures or some other house plan company? What about buying a small condominium or townhouse with a community yard and garden? Could you buy a place with land that you could (and would like) to make income producing? There are many, many possibilities for home ownership besides the conventional concept many of us have grown up with. Chapter 7 of *The Heart Has Its Own Reasons* is a good resource for reading about the different options, as are "alternate life-style" publications like *Mother Earth News* and the less glossy architecture magazines and plan catalogues. Keep in mind what your priorities are for family life in considering housing. For:

> there is something terribly sad about a residential street where house after house stands silent and empty during the day, heavily bolted against modern predators. The adults are out working—quite often to pay the high housing costs—and the children have been dispersed to various caretakers. Is the house serving the people, or are the people in service to the house? When parents and children are at home only in the evening and on weekends, *the tab for housing, per hour of its use, is very high*. In terms of enjoyment for the whole family, the return on the investment is truly low.[2]

In order for the mother to stay at home full- or part-time, many families simply rent an apartment for a little longer than they'd originally planned. But rents can be high, too, particularly in nice apartment complexes. Renting offers fewer alternatives than does home ownership, but there are still some options. I spoke to four women who lived in low-income housing subsidized by the federal government, by their city, and, in one case, by a combination of city, state, and federal funds. Two of these places were "not the greatest, but okay for a few years," the third was "nice—lots of young couples with kids and middle-aged divorced women with teenagers to baby-sit," the fourth was "super," located in a wooded area near an academic community.

In looking for this type of housing, you have to be careful, because some subsidized apartment complexes (or "projects") are favorite targets for vandalism, among other problems. But some can be very good, too. The best often have long waiting lists, so it's wise to get on the list as soon as you hear of a place.

One benefit in many apartment complexes that have lots of other families is that there are usually opportunities for baby-sitting exchanges, food cooperatives, and splitting the costs of everything from a daily newspaper to a side of beef.

In finding any place to rent that's reasonable for a one-paycheck family's budget, it is wise to ask around and check out all possibilities. Sometimes the best deal can be care-taking at a museum or living in the mammoth house of an elderly lady who spends half the year in Florida. These kinds of options are not available everywhere and I don't mean to suggest that they are. But there *are* innumerable possibilities for both renting and buying.

Reducing Medical Costs. After housing, medical and dental insurance and medical bills are big expenses that put dents in a good budget. You can either regard them as essentials and cut down somewhere else or you can look for alternatives. If you are near a university dental school, you can have routine checkups and cleanings done there and have more complicated procedures done by a dentist who's been in practice for many years. Considering the relatively low cost of toothpaste and dental floss, it's also a good idea to encourage strongly all family members to brush and floss often as well as to lay off sweets.

Because of recent changes in the health care field, people should look on health care as a "buyer's market." Doctors and hospitals are becoming more and more competitive. There are Health Maintenance Organizations (HMOs), urgent-care centers, shopping center doctors' offices, and health insurance HMOs, to name a few of the current options for health care. So you don't have to stick with the insurance policies and private physicians you may have had for years. If you are healthy and are not planning any more children, you can consider getting what I call "disaster insurance"—the minimum medical coverage for a disabling illness or accident. Visits to a doctor for a cold or the flu can be cut out by becoming knowledgeable about common symptoms and methods of relief. The expense of visits for an illness you are uncertain about can be kept down by going to a clinic with sliding scale fees. In some areas of the country, there are also health maintenance clinics run by Blue Cross/Blue Shield where the cost of well-baby visits and other routine office calls are reduced for insurance clients. If you have preschoolers, check out community health programs, which sometimes immunize young children free of charge or on a sliding scale.

It's also wise to practice "preventive medicine" at home by learning as much as possible about nutrition. It's fun and interesting if you teach your kids nutritional values as you learn them, cooking and making snacks together.

One tip about paying medical bills—or any bill, for that matter: if you have a problem paying a large bill, be forthright about your financial difficulties. Doctors, nurses, hospitals, and utility companies are providing you with services in good faith and expect to be paid in full promptly. If this isn't possible for you at some point, let them know immediately and set up a monthly payment plan that you can handle. A bookkeeper for a doctor once told me of a family of six that faithfully paid four dollars a month on a bill month after month. In such a situation, a medical office or utility will not send your name to a collection bureau as long as you pay each month. The practice to avoid is "letting a bill go," with the illusion that next month it will be easier to pay. After a few "next months," the bill collector may be beating on your door.

Speaking of bill collectors: many authors of books on economizing strongly recommend getting rid of credit cards, and I add my voice to the chorus. It's usually best to cancel all charges, keeping one or two charge cards for gasoline or a bank card to be used only in emergencies. Some families have card-cutting parties to celebrate the event.

Cutting Transportation Costs. In addition to saving on housing and medical and dental bills, my husband and I took a careful look at transportation expenses in trimming our household budget. We realized that millions of cars in North America sit idly in parking lots for eight hours a day, and that two of ours had been among them. We decided to sell the larger of our two cars. Two or three days a week my husband had the car we kept. On the other days I drove him twenty minutes to and from work so that I could have the car. Driving him was a pain in the neck, and yet it took only forty minutes out of a day that was otherwise mine. Later, he was sometimes able to get a ride to work with friends.

As two busy people sharing one car, we did experience frustrations and occasional arguments. But we saved so much in automobile insurance, repairs and maintenance, tires, and gasoline that it was worth it. We and the children learned to get to places riding bicycles and walking. We didn't buy a second car for four years, until the lack of a second car began to hinder my efforts to work part-time. We then spent a lot of time discussing the pros and cons, shopping around, and reading manuals. We finally bought a 1950 Ford that, unlike the other used cars in good shape that we could afford, would appreciate rather than depreciate in value over the years. It cost very little to insure and register and was technically simple enough for my husband to do some of his own maintenance on it with parts from a mail order house.

We found that there are many small ways to save in buying and running a car; most notably: changing your own oil, washing and waxing the vehicle yourself, pumping your own gas, and, if you don't have too complicated a car and can borrow the tools, doing the tune-up. I learned to be very gentle with my car; I would take my foot off the gas when I saw a stop sign ahead, for example, instead of continuing at the same speed and putting on the brakes just before the stop. This lengthened the life of the brakes in addition to saving gas. I also tried to discipline myself to fill the gas tank once every two weeks on payday. I wasn't rigid about this, especially if I could save money on an item by driving to a store having a sale. But I got so that I combined errand and food shopping within that two-week period and still had plenty of gas for weekend drives and enough to coast into the gas station on payday.

Saving on Fuel. We saved on fuel at home for our furnace by using a wood stove we'd installed years before as the primary instead of secondary source of heat. We took advantage of the fact that we live in an area that is heavily forested, buying green wood at only ninety dollars a cord every summer and letting it season in the backyard until fall. Initially, the stove heated only our kitchen, so we tore down the walls between it and the family room and breakfast area. We put a grate in the kitchen ceiling so that my study above was heated. Four rooms in our house are now heated with the wood stove, and another two we don't use much are heated moderately well. We wear a lot of layered clothing in fall and winter, and when the house gets unpleasantly cool in December or January, we turn on the furnace for supplemental heat.

Not everyone has—or wants to have—a wood stove for heat. But the point is that you can find savings on heat whether you live in the city or in the country. If nothing else, you can learn to dress differently.

Supplying the Family with Food. In our efforts to grow some of our own food, we had the problem many people do: very little land. Our front yard, which faces south, is five feet of asphalt, mostly owned by the city. But our backyard was large enough to cram in a 16' × 20' garden plot, a ragged but healthy row of raspberry bushes, and twelve strawberry plants that we got free with a vegetable seed order. Two years before I stopped working full-time we had planted dwarf peach and apricot trees in the side yard, and they began to be good producers the summer I quit. And surprisingly, all this food-producing vegetation still left room for a jungle gym and a small grassy area for the children to play in.

I am convinced that the important thing is not how much land you have; it's what you do with what you have, and being determined you will find a way to make it productive. I know of one woman who decided to stay home with her preschool child and also take art courses part-time in order to change careers when she eventually went back to work. She and her husband devised a number of ways to save money, but one of the most touching was the array of plastic tubs of tomato plants and other vegetables that helped fill out their sparsely furnished house as well as their daily menu. Someone who wants to quit full-time work badly enough and has just barely enough money to do it *can* find alternatives: food co-ops, container gardens on the roof, ethnic open markets, or sharing bulk orders with other families. The point is to look at a whole range of possibilities and ask yourself: "What am I doing with what I've got?"

I did find that there were some "side effects" connected to a few of our methods for saving money. For example, I hated the heat and fatigue involved in standing over a steaming pot of hot water in order to can the vegetables that came out of our prolific garden; they usually all got ripe during the hottest weeks of August and September. But I finally decided the sweat and strain were what my kids would call the "yucky" part of my new job. I had to put up with it.

For the grain products, cheese, and other products we could not grow in our garden, we joined a food co-op where I worked one hour a week. We also, of course, shopped at the local supermarket and drug store, and even there we learned to save. Instead of stopping at the shopping center every other day on my way home from work, I began shopping for food and other supplies once a week at night when my husband could stay with the kids. I could then go down the "no-brand" aisle without my children whining that they wanted a particular brand that was advertised on TV. And un-interrupted, I could do the mental arithmetic necessary to decide which of two brands or sizes was the most economical. By shopping alone, I could avoid arguing with my children about our buying Chocolat Bon-Bon Cereal or plastic prince and princess sets. I didn't need either the irritation or, when I gave in, the loss of revenue.

I once ran into a friend with her children in tow during an early evening trip to the supermarket. She looked at me enviously. "Oh," she said, "your husband is taking care of the kids so you can shop alone. How nice. Mine never takes them at night except for important stuff." I smiled and waved goodbye as her children dragged her away and I thought, *But this is serious stuff. I am spending money from an operating budget. This is business.*

A Food-buying Strategy. One of the best approaches to saving significantly at the supermarket is outlined in the book *Cut Your Grocery Bills in Half!* by consumer advocate Barbara Salsbury and writer Cheri Loveless. Their basic strategy is to plan meals and list foods carefully, to buy large amounts of the products you like when they're on special, and to stockpile like crazy. The book recommends using store brands rather than advertised national brands or (sometimes lower-quality) generic labels. And they caution against psychological lures and gimmicks.

Another word of caution about shopping specials: sometimes a market will have a big display *telling* you something is a great deal, so you buy ten of the item and come home to find that the supermarket where you usually buy that item sells it for ten cents *less*. It's a good idea to keep track of items you commonly buy and their lowest price in a pocket-sized notebook. Or type up a food and supply list with prices and keep it with you at all times, folded in a plastic sandwich bag to keep it from getting dog-eared.

Stockpiling canned goods and perishables seems impossible for anyone living in a small house or apartment. But even grains can be stored—by first freezing them (to kill all the critters lying dormant therein) and then stowing portions bagged in plastic in boxes at the back of a deep cupboard or under a double bed. Though the obvious criticism of this method is that few people have the money to buy large quantities in addition to their regular food items each week, the authors insist that it can be done by gradually using a bigger and bigger percentage of the grocery money to buy quantities of sale items. One way they suggest for starting is to plan meals for a week using up what you already have on hand so that much of your grocery budget for that week is freed for large quantity buying. Some families get started by using a birthday or Christmas check to buy store specials in bulk.

One big dividend to the plan Salsbury and Loveless outline in their book is that after a while you have such a good stock of food stashed under your bed that, except for fresh dairy products, you don't *have* to go to the store. According to Salsbury, if you have a financial or medical emergency you can use money usually budgeted for groceries to cover the emergency and still eat. Your stockpile just goes down.

Coupons and Bargains. In almost any discussion of food budgets, I find that sooner or later somebody asks me about couponing. Stories abound of "the 'coupon queens' who buy over $100 worth of groceries for a few dollars and a wad of coupons."[3] Over a hundred billion coupons are issued every year by a wide range of manufacturers.[4] They *can* save you money, especially if you use them in a store that's giving you double their printed worth. But it's important to remember that you can also lose money if you get something with a coupon that family members don't like, or if you buy an item that is more expensive than another brand even after you deduct the coupon savings. I don't know how many times I've picked up a brand of margarine that I had a coupon for, done a quick price comparison with the store brand I usually bought, and found that my usual brand was several cents cheaper. Manufacturers give consumers coupons "to promote three types of sales: getting people to try a new product, keeping old customers, and taking customers away from competitors."[5] Coupons are best used to buy products you know well, like giant boxes of your favorite laundry detergent. Other than that, use coupons with caution.

The difficulty with any good strategy is that it takes discipline and consistency to make it work. Sometimes the best money-saving methods in the world seem so tedious that it's hard to be consistent. However, the various methods really do need to be thought of as part of a business. When you give them "the thought, concern, and organization you [gave your career], you'll find the routineness wears off and ingenuity settles in."[6]

Whenever anyone says to me or to another at-home mother, "But with all your education, doesn't it bother you that you aren't using your mind?" I can rarely keep myself from laughing outright. For those of us in families with a middle or lower-middle income, never have we had to use our minds more. I became better at creative problem solving after two years at home than I was after six years of higher education. As a mother at home, I had to resist the temptation to solve a problem with money and instead had to think up as many solutions as I could. I really had to think.

Developing a Positive Attitude

All the methods of saving described in the various commercial, governmental, university, and community publications you can get are greatly enhanced by your having the right attitude. What I did in a small New England city, parents in Manhattan or Los Angeles perhaps could not do. But they might be able to do things that I couldn't. Determination and commitment to simplicity contribute a lot to saving money no matter where you live.

When our family discussed—sometimes fought about—things we wanted to buy on our limited budget, we had to concentrate on what our priorities were. We had all agreed that we wanted to have me at home. This was an emotional luxury that we'd agreed was more important than some of the material luxuries we could have had if I'd continued working. An important thing to remember after a few years of living on a shoestring budget is that it won't last forever. Most of us eventually go back to work to save for our children's education or simply because we want to have a regular outside job again. In the meantime there are lots of freebies out there to enjoy.

6

How to Be As Happy at Home As You'd Hoped to Be

BEING happy at home is easy for some women who've been in the working-mom rat race for years and are glad to get out, or, never having been in it, are proud of their choice to stay home and enjoy it fully. I, for one, had no adjustment problems. But this isn't true for everyone. In her book *Where's My Happy Ending?*, Lee Morical points out that today

> we are confronted by a . . . scenario in which marriage [and motherhood] are pictured as the answer to "saving" a woman from life on the fast track by once again returning her to the comforting warmth of the hearth. . . . It can be tremendously fulfilling. But like the job outside the home, it can never be *the* answer.[1]

Life at home, especially with babies and preschoolers, has its own pressures and hassles.

But there are some things you can do for yourself that will give you a good chance of being very happy at home: 1) get your identity and priorities straight, 2) find inexpensive ways to enjoy life by yourself, with your spouse and friends, and with your children, and 3) clarify to your children, in-laws, and friends what your values and priorities are.

The first task is not easy to accomplish with the heavy emphasis today on the question "And what do you do?" I once went to a brunch on a spring Sunday morning after I'd been up half the night with my son, and encountered this question when I was feeling rather irritable. When I went up to the buffet table shortly after our arrival, I noticed a young woman leaning on the bookcase next to the table, sipping a Bloody Mary. She had long, frizzy permed hair and long brown-lacquered fingernails and was wearing a long, thin, cinnamon-colored jumpsuit. We exchanged pleasantries about the food and the flowers on the table, and then I introduced myself. After giving me her name, she asked, "What do you do?" with a heavy emphasis on the *do*. I didn't want to say I was a housewife because I felt that I was much more a mother and a wife than a *house*wife. I didn't feel like telling her I was a *former* writing teacher, and there was something about the woman that made me feel uncomfortable about saying what I *had* been doing just hours before: cleaning up a little child who'd been throwing up half the night.

So I told the young woman with the long brown nails that I ran a twenty-four-hour-a-day child care center. Her eyes bugged out behind her mascaraed lashes.

"Twenty-four hours? Are *you* on call twenty-four hours?"

I assured her that I was because I was the director of the center. In fact, I was on call twenty-four hours a day, seven days a week.

"Oh, it must be a demanding job," the woman breathed.

"Yes," I chuckled. "Worse than being a pediatrician."

"But a challenge, right?"

"Right!"

A psychologist I consulted in writing this book, who does part-time counseling and is a gifted craftswoman, answers the question "What do you do?" with a satisfied, "I'm at home with my children." If someone else in the room asks to borrow her doctoral dissertation or asks whether she sold a lot at the craft fair last weekend, she will certainly talk about those things. But her primary work is raising her children, so this is her initial answer.

One woman said that she always says "I'm at home with kids" and then goes on to elaborate on all the free time she spends at the beach and at museums, the clothes she designs and makes, the stained glass course she's taking, the bike rides she enjoys every afternoon with her children. "I don't stop until I see that their eyes are green with envy. After all, they wanted to know what I *do*."

So, before you come face to face with this situation, decide what your standard answer is going to be to the "do" question and say it with pride and satisfaction. *How* we state our occupation makes a difference in the way we think about ourselves and in the way others perceive us. It is a little silly to say, "I'm a domestic engineer." We don't need to dress up the job. Besides, pushing paper at an office is no more noble than pushing a broom and wiping noses at home. So be glad if you're an at-home mother with only the one job, and sound like it!

Actually, if someone were to write a job description for a wife and mother of young children it would vie with that of a corporate executive: "Demanding, intense work; long hours, especially during the first two to five years; extensive responsibility, but unlimited possibilities for creativity. After six to eight years on the job, employee has six hours a day to pursue creative, intellectual, or recreational interests; part-time help with household chores after 3:00 P.M. will also be available at this time." This is not a bad deal at all, especially when you consider that all the bear hugs and sticky kisses you get aren't even included in this job description, and that's the best part of all.

Keep in mind, too, that at-home mothers may be a growing majority. Fifty-five percent of the women who had babies in 1982 did not reenter the labor force after a year at home. According to sociologist Amitai Etzioni, there is currently a trend toward professional women leaving their careers to remain at home with their children.[2]

Setting Priorities

But it is really up to us to make the job a good one. It is easy to get caught up in household work and in small people's needs. When children are babies, there is no way to get around this. But that period can be enjoyable, and once it's over you can move on to other things. It's important to figure out what you *want* to do; in other words, set priorities. As one writer-housewife put it:

Review what the job entails and choose from among its components which to keep [and] which to forget. *Forget* the laundry, the cooking and cleaning and the decorating because I [do] that too, on the side. . . .[3] More than anything else, I think this is the secret of home making: creating a place that makes people feel good. . . . It means creating a home where people will want to linger over dinner; where they will want to snuggle up with a quilt and a book on a rainy day instead of escaping to the shopping mall. What it does not mean is spending all day long with a can of Lysol in our hands.[4]

Making physical changes in our lives (like quitting a full-time job) does not necessarily mean that our lives will change unless *we* change. If you were trying to be a Superwoman as a working mother, you can try the same trick as a mother at home. Depression is common in housewives. Some of this depression is caused by the low value the housewife's job is given by society, but it can also be caused by women's trying to be perfectionists in a job that has no end. It can also be caused by poor time management. The following suggestions can give you a good start on getting rid of both problems:

Set a schedule.

Get out of the house.

Assign tasks to your children.

Be assertive about your needs.

Get rid of the notion that you must be perfect. No one is, so if that's your goal, you're bound to fail.

Finally, keep your sense of humor. It's everyone's best weapon against stress.[5]

Adapting to At-Home Mothering

When Arlene Cardozo, the author of *Woman at Home*, was a young mother living in Cambridge, Massachusetts, she helped organize a newcomers' group at Harvard in 1965, made up of women from all regions of the United States. While doing this, she investigated why some young mothers were happy at home and some were not by comparing their attitudes.

[Happy women] did what was necessary . . . not a speck of dust more. This allowed each woman to distinguish between housework—much of which was unimportant—and the care of her children, which was of prime importance to her. . . . One sharp contrast was that the woman who enjoyed being at home used her ingenuity and creativity to retain existing interests or to develop new ones while at home, but the woman who was unhappy at home often could not function productively away from school or office without someone else to give her assignments and deadlines. It never occurred to her to find new ways to use her abilities, if being at home precluded her doing things in old ways. Nor did she develop new interests if old ones couldn't fit into her new routine.[6]

Elsewhere in her book, Arlene Cardozo laments that the women's movement in the 1960s and 1970s "did not support the woman at home by helping her to *alter* the causes of her boredom and loneliness."[7] Instead, getting an outside job was encouraged. But as many of us found out, doubling the work load is no help. Much more important is establishing your own priorities.

Getting Organized

I found that the most important part in finding fulfillment and happiness at home was organizing my life around my priorities. I made a list of general priorities and interests like writing and spending time with the kids, and then sometimes I would also have a daily list of priorities, like getting some curtains measured and cut or picking tomatoes before they rotted in the garden. The housework was never on a priority list, yet it was a responsibility I had to meet. Eventually I devised a method for doing household chores that I have since dubbed the "incidental system of housework."

As usual, I would decide each evening or early in the morning what I wanted most to do on a particular day. After that I would write down what I *had* to do, like doing three loads of laundry and the usual kitchen chores. The first thing I would do in the morning after getting the children fed was to organize the laundry and do one load. After playing with my son and getting him interested in a game he could play by himself or with a neighbor friend, I would do the thing I cared most about, interrupting myself for nothing, including the sound of the washing machine's concluding spin. Later, I would take a break, putting the clean clothes on the line and starting a second load of laundry. Around dinner time I might get the third load of laundry into the washer and dryer and later ask my husband to fold. By the end of the day, I would have taken care of the laundry, but I would have spent very little physical and psychic energy on it.

Now that my children are older and in school, I don't have any more interruptions that can't be ignored, so I get even more done. But my house certainly does not look beautifully tended by a full-time housewife with six hours each day to do housework. Daily chores like dish washing get done when I'm in the kitchen preparing meals. So I wash breakfast dishes when I'm taking a tea break at 10:30 or warming up leftovers for lunch. Lunch and snack dishes get taken care of while I'm preparing dinner. Dinner dishes are either done for me by small hands or else my husband or I do them when we're talking to the kids about their homework at night. Laundry gets sorted and folded when I'm taking a break from editing a manuscript; the phone gets dusted when I'm talking on it; mending gets done when I'm talking to my children about how their day went at school.

In short, the chores are incidental to what's really important in my life. I don't know why this method of organizing work gives me so much more time than most people seem to have, but it does and *somehow* my responsibilities to the house and the family are met by the end of each week. Well, most weeks.

Using Your "Prime Time." Another method I've discovered that helps me get what I want out of being at home is to think about what part of my day is "prime time" for attending to my own special interests. When the children were little, "prime time" was nap time and an hour or two during "Sesame Street" and "Mr. Rogers." Now it's when they are at school, watching cartoons on Saturday morning, or outside playing with friends.

But "prime time" is also when I'm at *my* prime. I am definitely a morning person, so that's when I need to do anything that requires concentration or a lot of creative energy. I discovered this one Saturday morning when I was paying bills and felt frustrated and stymied, with a lot of nervous energy. I realized that I was writing checks and licking envelopes—something I could do half asleep—when I was full of energy to dig in the garden or paint the front door. Now I schedule my day so that I do interesting, energy-consuming tasks in the morning. I use the afternoons for quiet times with my children, shopping, bill paying, vacuuming, or a short nap. I find that I'm a lot more in tune with myself physically and mentally and not as tired at the end of a full day.

If you dislike housework, be sure you don't schedule it during either type of prime time or you will begin feeling like a drudge. And, if your children are three years old or older, be sure to start them young helping you around the house. Encourage their natural desire to "be grown-up and help." You can give them your own tools or get miniature brooms, mops, and snow shovels at yard sales or from willing grandparents who will buy them.

Getting Children to Help. Once kids are school-aged, there is a great deal more that they can do to help. At this point it's important to think of yourself as "the manager, not the maid"[8] and delegate responsibilities. According to one writer, "Family members need to understand that a mother has limits of time and energy, and that the family's efforts to help with order will free her to do things that will benefit everyone."[9]

Let it be known that everybody has to take his or her part in doing the "yuck chores." Even small children can understand elementary concepts of fairness, and obviously it would be terribly unfair for only one person—you—to do all the work. Here are some tips for getting people in your family to help:

Explain to family members that you're an equal opportunity employer.

Discuss your household situation honestly and calmly. Determine what needs to be done daily, weekly, monthly.

If thorough cleaning is impossible each week, set priorities and decide what *must* be done.

Decide how work can be divided. Is there a logical person to do certain tasks, based on preference, ability, or time?

After agreeing on this division, make lists of each person's particular duties. This clarifies what needs to be done, serves as a reminder to do it, and eliminates "I forgot" as an excuse.

Be sure family members know how to do various tasks and be willing to teach.

Consider setting aside a specific time—an hour on Saturday perhaps—when everyone pitches in. A "we're all in this together" approach can encourage cooperation.

Be flexible and willing to experiment. If one method of sharing chores doesn't work, try another.

Don't criticize if tasks aren't done exactly to your standards. Keep comments constructive and instructive.

Remember that humor helps. Nagging is counterproductive.[10]

If your children are too small to help or for some other reason you don't have the assistance you need, figure out a way to get help—team up with a friend to clean at each other's houses a few hours a week, exchange specific cleaning chores with a friend or neighbor, find a willing high school or college student, hire a retarded adult who's had janitorial training, hire a professional cleaner for a half or full day if you can afford it, or, if you can't afford it, for two hours a week squeezed onto the beginning of another customer's full or half day.

Whether you get outside help or not, use all the resources available to help you become more efficient at home. Check out the books in the library that have suggestions for managing time. Some of these are geared for mothers at home, and some of them are for women working full-time. I use them all. They have tips on everything, from installing a phone with a long cord in your kitchen so that you can cook while you talk with friends, to rubbing the runners of drawers with candle wax so they won't stick. They all discourage mothers from becoming slaves to their children.

If you ever have the temptation to straighten the messy room of a school-age or teenage child, figuring "I just work part-time" or "I'm home all the time now," find a cold washcloth and slap it across your face. The child can do the room alone or with *assistance* from you. If you want to do something for your children, bake cookies as a snack when they come home from school or take time for a long talk together over ice cream cones. These are the kinds of things that make memories for them. Remember, you are working full-time as a mother, a maker of Home, a shaper of young lives.

Do the basics, keep the place sanitary, and save as much money as you can by doing things the old-fashioned way, but most of all, enjoy the job. When you're not enjoying it because of an overdose, find someone to look after your children for an hour or more and get out.

Getting Out of the House. Here is one piece of advice that I heard many times and did not act on often enough. Sometimes a community can help you to get out of the house. There are now senior citizen and church-sponsored Mother's Day Out services for young mothers, to which you can bring your baby or preschooler for an entire morning once a week. There are also baby-sitting co-ops in many areas. If there isn't one where you live, you can start one. Or organize a play group (see appendix A). People are usually attracted pretty quickly. And, if you can afford it, there are many nursery schools in most areas, offering a wide range of prices and programs. One fringe benefit to any of these possibilities is that if you don't know many other at-home mothers, you can meet them through your children's participation in a group.

There are also women who have started Mother's Day Out services as a business, similar to home day care but only one morning a week. Sometimes the fifteen or twenty dollars they make while mothers go out is used to purchase their *own* time out.

Networking. Another way of overcoming isolation or loneliness is through "networking"—getting together regularly with women to exchange ideas and experiences. Businesswomen have been doing this for years, not only for business referrals but also to overcome *their* loneliness. Many mothers' networks grow out of a church or other existing group. But you can also start one yourself with a free ad in a nonprofit newsletter, shopper's flyer, or with a 3″ × 5″ notice on a supermarket bulletin board. In networks, mothers meet at each others' houses or at low-cost community space once a week or once a month. Usually one mother looks after the children while the other mothers socialize and exchange information.

Baby-sitting Exchanges. Though none of these aids in getting out were available to me when my children were young (and I was working a good deal of that time), I did set up "baby-sitting exchanges" with neighbors and friends. Usually we used these for just a few hours of free time, but occasionally we exchanged children for a whole weekend when the kids felt comfortable with the idea. Now that they are older, we do this more often.

Recreation. When I go out for a couple of hours by myself, I do things like walking on the beach or window-shopping. Every now and then, I go to a poetry reading or an art film with a friend. These are all fun or soul nourishing or both and they cost nothing. They are my own brand of "cheap thrills."

My husband and I also have our "cheap thrills." Almost every Saturday night we go out on a "date." If we have money, we go to a movie or to a nice place for dessert. If we don't, we go "cruising" down Main Street in our 1950 Ford or out on the highway that leads into the country. We usually are alone on our "dates" and use a lot of the time to catch up on what we're doing and how we're feeling.

In finding inexpensive recreation to enjoy with your children, Bonnie Watkins, a contributor to the newsletter *Welcome Home,* suggests that families take advantage of the community:

> Visit a pet store, a car wash, a bakery, an airport. . . . Look for free exhibits and displays at shopping malls, reduced movie prices at bargain matinees, public library programs. Learn which recreation centers and museums offer free programs for children. Frequent the public playgrounds, parks, and swimming pools instead of expensive summer camps. Check community school classes (usually a few dollars tuition) for courses children can take.[11]

She also suggests that you avoid the toy store and have children play with simple, nonbreakable household items like pots and pans. I found that if I had my children watch mostly public television instead of commercial TV programs, their whining for new toys was lessened because they didn't see them advertised. I have never been very good about setting up creative projects for my children every day, but I did have them draw and color a great deal. Bonnie Watkins suggests that if you use lots of paper at your house, call a company that uses computers and ask if you can pick up their used paper. You can get decorative paper for wrapping birthday presents and for crafts by asking wallpaper store owners for their canceled wallpaper books.

The local public library has magazines and books for children that have recipes for making play dough, finger paints, corn starch "goo," and bubble soap as well as instructions for making things out of string, yarn, and cloth remnants. You can also send away for lots of freebies (see appendix A).

Gift Buying

We encouraged our kids to make instead of buy Christmas and other gifts. Even before I quit work the children had enjoyed making gifts so we made this a yearly practice at Christmas time. One year we got kits with coloring markers and "plate papers" to color on, which we then sent to a craft company in Texas where the drawings were incorporated into plastic plates. Another year we gave cups made in the same way and the year after that, I had the children draw designs on cloth napkins with fabric paints.

When we buy Christmas presents at a store instead of making them, we have a set budget, say, five dollars a person. The children take time to make these very thoughtful presents. Though they might want to buy a sweater for a grandma or a twenty-dollar golf book for a favorite uncle, they will wind up instead with a small photo album with pictures of themselves selected for it or "World's Greatest" printed on a plain T-shirt. As corny as it may sound, we truly have found that these presents, whether made or bought, have helped us understand what giving is all about. Maybe because the children are giving a lot of themselves in deciding on them. As far as the relatives and friends receiving them are concerned, creativity and care make up for what we lack monetarily, and the gifts have been a big hit.

For gifts within the family, we also have a budget. Often my husband and I buy a series of small presents for each other that are only two or three dollars apiece. They may include something like bakery bread, or imported sour candies, luxuries we wouldn't ordinarily buy that are relatively inexpensive. In buying for both ourselves and our children, we pay with cash or by check only. We never charge anything or "borrow" from the savings account. To manage this, we start buying things for the children in late summer or we let money build up in the checking account and buy everything in November and December. Obviously, we can't buy many expensive things paying only in cash, but everybody understands this. We start singing the old Shaker song " 'Tis a Gift to be Simple" around the house even before Halloween hits, and by Christmas, the message has sunk in for our kids.

Learning to Live with Less

There have been times when not having much money at Christmastime— and plenty of other times—has been a source of frustration to me. I was surprised to find that our house helped me to keep things in perspective. I had always cursed the inadequacies of our old house: the outdated plumbing, the shallow closets, and the bizarre lighting arrangements that had been installed in the early 1900s. I can't say I had a Zen conversion to peace and serenity the first year or so at home, but I did learn a great deal from my venerable house in spite of myself.

One thing that had especially annoyed me about the house was that the closets—what few there were—had a depth of only about twelve or fifteen inches. Instead of a pole for hangers there was only a strip of wood in the back studded with old-fashioned hooks and rosehead nails. In the one little closet in our bedroom my clothes were hung in layers on the hooks. I realized one day that these few hooks had seemed quite adequate when they'd been put up because the eighteenth- and nineteenth-century occupants of the house hadn't had many clothes to hang up. Thereafter, instead of cursing the inadequacies of the closet, I tried to concentrate on the fact that I had an awful lot of clothes to hang up.

In *The Success Ethic and the Shattered American Dream*, author Blaine Taylor reminds us that even a low- or moderate-income American is relatively rich compared with people of other eras and other regions of the world:

> Music, news, and every variety of cultural input is constantly available. Almost everyone has a camera. One hundred years ago, not even the richest king could look at the pictures of his children and of his grandchildren, and relive the past highlights of his life with clear images memory had not dimmed or forgotten. . . . At the turn of a switch or dial, almost any American may watch a man step on the moon or visit the Grand Canyon. He may enjoy from across a continent a sporting event or a Broadway play.
>
> In a world of famine and shortage, most Americans have fresh meat, fruits, and vegetables out of season. . . . Americans eat better than kings did in previous centuries.[12]

Obviously, in the midst of a staggering array of material goods, many of us forget these facts. One thing that helped me to remember, apart from my old house, was reading other books like Taylor's: *The Future Is Not What It Used to Be: Returning to Traditional Values in an Age of Scarcity*, *Voluntary Simplicity*, and *Small is Beautiful*. I also reread Laura Ingalls Wilder's Little House books with my six-year-old the year I quit. Times change and people change, but we *can* do without and survive.

As children get older and begin to have more expensive material wants, it can be difficult to explain why they cannot have things that some children acquire with apparent ease. Sometimes it helps simply to explain in clear language why there isn't much money and why it is important to you to stay home. But this period in your children's lives may signal the time for you to get an outside full-time job or to expand an existing part-time home business—that is, if your children's wants are important to *you*. If they aren't, sometimes it's better to help children figure out how to get things they want themselves: through their own part-time job, an allowance savings plan, or a yard sale.

As a result of our talks about this kind of thing, my almost-twelve-year-old daughter purchased "Baby-Sitter" business cards in preparation for the day she could baby-sit. My son gathered together old skates, his bike, and some nearly new toys one Saturday morning, printed "For Sale" signs on cardboard for passersby to see, and sat in the driveway for longer than he'd have liked until he made sixty dollars.

I have always worried that not having a lot of material things or having to work so hard themselves in order to buy them would make my children grow up to be materialists. A few years ago, I was worrying about this quite a bit during the Christmas season, hoping that the early foundation we had laid and the efforts we'd made to let our children know what mattered most to us would have a lasting influence on them. But I wasn't sure. My daughter at that time (age eight) had rejected PBS educational programs and was watching two hours of commercial TV every afternoon, with its barrage of Christmas commercials for toys and dolls every ten minutes. She frequently called me in to see a commercial for something she "especially wanted," which was just about everything. She was wise to the fact that Momma was Santa Claus.

I finally sat her down one evening when the television was shut off and told her that her grandparents were already getting two of the big things she wanted. Her father and I would give her the usual stocking stuffers and small things and *one* large present. I wanted her to calm down and think.

"Of all the things you could have, what one thing do you want the most for Christmas?"

"What do I want the *most?*"

"Yes."

She seemed to relax a bit as if this simplified everything and then she looked very serious. "Most of all, I want . . . I want *world peace!*"

Enough said. I decided that maybe she wouldn't grow up to be a materialist after all.

7

Building Bridges

SOME women find that no matter how happy they are at home or how diligently they work at economizing, there comes a time when they feel they must go back to work, either full- or part-time. Recently, there has been a lot of scare talk about how disastrous it is for a woman to stay out of work for more than a short time. The following is typical:

> It is important to know that as a woman you will beyond doubt have to work for money to support yourself a large part of your life and to do that you will need skills, and that if you stay home for much more than a year your skills will need retooling.[1]

Except for jobs in high tech and the medical field, this description is quite an exaggeration. I'd amend "a year" to "five years" for most of us. For the woman who takes courses in her field now and then during the years she's home, serves in a professional organization, or does volunteer work related to her field or applicable elsewhere, I'd add a few more years. What's more, we learn a tremendous amount at home and often acquire new skills that are later marketable. Before I stayed home with my children I had only two marketable skills: writing and teaching. After six years at home, I now have some others: wallpapering, painting, and light carpentry.

In discussing this issue, it's also important to keep in mind that "the average worker under thirty-five years of age goes about job hunting once every one-and-a-half years! And the average worker over thirty-five, once every three years."[2] Granted, the job hunting cited in such general statistics includes unattractive, nonprofessional jobs as well as the more attractive positions you might seek, but the fact remains: workers in the United States change their employment often. The days of the worker who stays at a firm all or even half his or her working life are fast fading. Therefore, if you choose to become a mother and home manager for several years, you really won't be any different from any other worker. Society doesn't yet see it this way, but you can avoid many of the problems inherent in this fact if *you* view motherhood as a job as well as a pleasure and responsibility. There are ways to write a résumé and generally present yourself that can maximize what you have to offer a potential employer.

Part- or Full-Time?

The first thing you have to do is decide when you want to work for pay again and whether it should be part-time or full-time. Full-time work is usually 9 to 5, but there are some employers, such as hospitals, who will let you work an early morning or evening shift so that your husband or someone else can fill in during the hours when your children are awake and you're away. If you can still get time alone with your spouse, this can work well.

In both full- and part-time work, a wide range of possible hours is now developing in the work place. Among the most common are:

Mothers' hours, which parallel local school hours.

V-time, in which workers agree in writing to shorten their hours by as much as 50 percent for six months to a year. They keep their benefits and position, but have reduced incomes commensurate with the reduction in hours. At the end of the prescribed period, employees return to full-time hours or renegotiate their hours. (This is a good system for a new mother who can't afford to quit, but is unhappy at the idea of having only six or eight weeks with her new baby. Unfortunately, it's highly unusual outside California and New York.)

Regular part-time, which usually means between ten and thirty-two hours of work a week. The more hours you work, the more likely it is that you will get benefits.

Flexible time, Flex-time, Flexi-time, all of which refer to full-time work but on a schedule that's best for the individual: 7:00 A.M. to 3:00 P.M. every day, or 9 to 5 three days a week and a long weekend, or . . . the possibilities are endless. Some employers willing to set up flex-time do insist on certain "core days" or "core hours," meaning that you have to be there every Monday morning, let's say, because important staff meetings are held then.[3]

These are all possibilities for the woman who is returning to work after being out of the work force for awhile, as well as for the woman who has a full-time job and wants to alter the hours. Some job counselors specializing in these new ways to work suggest that if you wish to return to the work force or enter for the first time, you should look for jobs that interest you, even if they have conventional full-time hours. Once you've been offered the job, present a strong case for tailoring the hours to your needs and negotiate with your potential new boss. For more on this, see the section in this chapter on job sharing.

Negotiating with a Present Employer

If you are now in the working-mom rat race, but are certain that you cannot afford to quit completely, talk to your present boss. There are many employers who simply *do not know* how difficult it is for a woman with small children to juggle everything. After all, things *look* all right, and everybody in the media seems to be saying that it is. In fact, there are now many articles in women's magazines that chronicle the stresses and strains, but employers— often still men—don't read women's magazines. So they frequently have no conception of the problems. Also, if they're the kind of men who think that housewives and mothers don't *do* anything all day, then the media image of the working woman who easily blends all her responsibilities helps to compound their basic prejudices.

Therefore, if you want to continue at a particular job, but with reduced hours, you must clearly, frankly explain how difficult things now are for you. Believe it or not, your boss may not know unless you tell him or her. I was surprised to find that when I started writing about the difficulties of juggling home, job, and family, colleagues from the university where I had taught would make comments like, "You are the last working mother I would have thought was having problems." Obviously, I faked it well. Keep in mind that you may too without realizing it. As with so many things, communication is essential. You will get nowhere if you keep your mouth shut.

Job Hunting—Presenting the Skills You've Gained as a Housewife

If, on the other hand, you are one of those people who's been out of the work force for several years or you've never worked outside the home, don't feel that you haven't got a chance to land anything but a low-paying, low-status job. One writer found that "employers value the sense of responsibility and the experience in getting along with people that a mature woman has."[4] I interviewed the highly successful manager of a branch office of a large company based in Ohio who, during her years at home had done extensive volunteer work, taught adult education classes, and briefly worked as a legal secretary. Rather than leave a gap of several years on her résumé, this dynamic and forceful woman listed her volunteer positions on her résumé and described the many organizational skills she had acquired. The experiences we gain in planning, managing, and budgeting in the process of raising a family are nothing for anyone to look askance at. One study estimated that eighty-eight skills are used by housewives in their role; some of these are marketable skills.[5]

The trick is to make them look as impressive to a potential employer as they really are. Remember that in résumés you list what you have *done*, not whether the work was full- or part-time. You must, of course, explain what work was part-time or volunteer during an interview. But by then, you have "one foot in the door." If a part-time task was a consistent, important contribution to an organization or business, do not undermine it or you by listing it as part-time on your résumé.

The sample résumé in the job-sharing section that follows lists "free-lance copy editor, 1978–83" for one woman and "editor, *Tides*, 1979–85" for the other woman. These were part-time positions for small community newsletters during the years my fictitious editors stayed at home with small children. But I saw no need to state this on the résumé.

When writing your résumé, present everything you've done positively. If you've organized a play group for the neighborhood or built a greenhouse out of old storm windows, present these as skills. "Employers will take it seriously as long as you take it seriously and communicate exactly what you've been able to accomplish."[6]

Here is an example of how one mother said she would describe her job if she were looking for a job:

> Responsible for the management of a 2,000 square foot facility. Schedule and supervise daily activities and education of two preschoolers. Constantly utilize my organizational and management skills and knowledge of child development. Able to work in chaotic environment with few breaks. Required to be patient, creative, and resourceful. Qualified for similar management position outside the home.[7]

If you need help in writing a résumé and cover letters, take out the appropriate books and manuals from your public library (for a book with specific examples, see appendix A). Make your résumé succinct—a page is good—but also detailed. Try to see a career counselor who specializes in women who are reentering the work force if you are especially nervous. Also, do some role-play interviewing with your husband or a good friend. Once you have a résumé written and some confidence, give out the résumé to friends and acquaintances who seem appropriate, either for giving advice or for helping you make contacts. More jobs are found through personal contact than through the want ads.

One way to find employment is by applying for a job (or devising a job yourself) for a school, church, synagogue, hospital, or organization where you have volunteered. I know of one newly divorced mother of two who got a three-quarter-time job at a hospital where she had volunteered for years. Another woman who had trouble making ends meet after the birth of her second child got a job teaching Hebrew in her congregation for ten dollars an hour a few hours a week. So, look around and ask around. Volunteer work may not seem like an obvious option because it is unpaid work, but it is valuable and can lead to other things.

Staying in Contact

Many women who quit their jobs to stay home with children do not have much to do with their profession or former colleagues after they leave. Sometimes this can be a big mistake. First, being at home with little children, though fun and stimulating, can get wearing. It's good to have adult stimulation and conversation now and then with someone other than an adult you live with. A successful entrepreneur suggests that you drop in occasionally at your old job at the end of a day or at lunch. The opportunity for a part-time or job-sharing position can sometimes turn up in such casual visits. Keeping up contacts will enable you to build, not burn, the bridges behind you.

If your former job—or a profession you're interested in getting into—has a professional organization, consider joining it. Keeping a membership in such an organization usually costs only pennies a week and is another good way to maintain old friendships and to gain knowledge about developments in your field. You may not care as much as you once did about the latest tax laws, the best whirlpool for physical therapy patients, or how to teach English as a second language, but keep up the professional membership anyway. If your professional organization publishes a newsletter or journal, maintain your subscription and read it occasionally. Consider becoming an officer, too. One woman I interviewed who was a job sharer became an officer in her professional organization after her twins were born and she was home. She found having that professional affiliation and holding an office resulted in having her name better known after she quit than when she was working full-time. It also contributed to her finding a good position when she wanted to return to work and locating another professional to share the position.

If you have no professional affiliation but are a college graduate, consider joining AAUW (American Association of University Women). A good feminist organization to join is NOW (National Organization for Women), for contrary to what many may think, NOW has housewives in its membership. Eleanor Smeal, twice president of NOW was a housewife for years and has championed "homemaker's rights."

If the years have gone by and you haven't kept up old contacts or made new ones, it's certainly not too late. You can join organizations now. If you've lost contact or moved away from your old job-hunting ground, that's okay too. Contact night schools and organizations like the YWCA to see what courses and workshops are available on reentering the labor force. Find out what opportunities there are in your area for networking and make contact with other women who've returned to part-time or full-time work after years of being at home. If you feel you lack self-confidence, do what you can to build it by learning as much as possible about the field you're interested in so you'll feel knowledgeable in interviews. For psychic bolstering, enlist the emotional support of friends and family, give yourself pep talks in the mirror, get a new haircut—whatever will give you a boost.

Opportunities for Part-Time Work Outside the Home

Because raising children is a job in itself, even when they reach school age, many women prefer to find part-time jobs. Therefore, the remainder of this chapter concentrates on part-time opportunities outside the home. Chapter 8 focuses on part-time paying work at home.

Contrary to what many people think, there are thousands of job possibilities for part-time work. One-fifth of the jobs available in the United States today are part-time. The Work in America Institute has estimated that in the late 1980s, tremendous growth will take place in part-time opportunities.[8] Poll taker Daniel Yankelovich has called part-timers and others involved in alternative work styles the "New Breed."

In deciding what exactly you want to do part-time, it's a good idea to assess your marketable skills, the jobs that are available, and what you like doing. There are many, many resources available to help you do this (see appendix A for further readings).

It's particularly important to pay attention to what I call personal quirks. Are you a morning person or a night person? Do you like steady work for a fixed number of hours a day, the same days each week, or do you thrive on change and variety? Do you work well in spurts, twenty minutes here, five minutes there? Or do you like to work for long, intense periods under pressure for a few days and then have complete freedom for several days? Are you a high-, average-, or low-energy sort of person? Do you want a "bread and butter" job that will simply help feed your family well, or do you want a professional career? Do you want to learn new skills, or do you prefer to do the same type of work you did before having children?

While we're on the subject, it's important to consider the quirks and personalities of your baby/child/children. Do you have children who feel pretty confident and happy when you're not around? Do you have access to a really good sitter or a relative your children love to be with? If not, would your spouse or other adults you live with look after your children in the evening, or would this be too exhausting for them?

Sometimes child care by people outside the family can be avoided completely by concocting a combination of short-term jobs, some of which you do at home when your children are playing, in school, or asleep, and some of which you do outside the home with your children in tow or while they're at home with a relative or spouse. For example, the writer for the "Making Money at Home" feature in the newsletter *Welcome Home* describes doing everything from political analysis for a presidential campaign to updating mailing lists to market research to candy tasting. Some of these things she did at home with her children nearby, and some she did alone outside the home in the evenings or during school hours. A combination of individual short-term jobs requires organizational skills, a sense of humor, and an interest in constantly keeping an eye out for possible jobs. Some people thrive on this method of making money part-time, and others say that they would go crazy fast doing it.

Obviously, there are lots of things to think about. It's a mistake to feel that evaluating them all is not worthwhile because the job will be "just" part-time. There is nothing inconsequential about how you spend ten to thirty hours of your life each week. So take time to evaluate your individual situation and the possibilities for work.

"Group Permanent Part-Time." As a result of several social and economic developments today, there is a wide range of part-time work available. A growing area of clerical part-time work is what is called "group permanent part-time" where a group of workers all work part-time shifts, often receiving the same hourly pay as full-time workers and, if they work more than twenty hours a week, usually one-half the benefits. These jobs are permanent, and because you work within a group of other part-timers there is a sense of camaraderie and continuity that some part-time jobs lack. Banks,

hospitals, insurance companies, data-processing firms, schools, retail stores, the food industry, and the U.S. government have such groups of part-time workers.

Temporary Office Work. One type of part-time work that has been around for years is temporary office work. Traditionally, temporary agencies were the only places where you could get these jobs, and such agencies are still a very good source. But something new in this field is the increase in "temp banks" run by large companies or firms. Their personnel departments create a group or "bank" of temporary workers whom they recruit and call on as needed. Because no intermediary agency is involved, you can sometimes make more money than you would at a temporary agency. These "banks" are made up of former employees, well-recommended friends, and people answering want ads who have the clerical or bookkeeping skills the company requires.

Both the newer and the traditional types of temporary work are good for a mother with young children because if someone has an ear infection on the day you get a call for work, you can say no and the next person on the list is called. The national temporary agencies like Kelly and Manpower are still good and have improved over the years in some important areas. They now offer a variety of positions in addition to secretarial and clerical jobs, can sometimes give you pay close to or equal to that of permanent employees, and offer their own benefits packages. Kelly and Olsten also offer training and retraining programs, which can be a big help to anyone who's been out of the labor force for awhile or was never in it.

Professional and Semiprofessional Jobs. Increasingly, there are also professional and semiprofessional jobs available part-time. Approximately two million men and women are involved in such positions, including nurses, doctors, economists, lawyers, statisticians, writers, computer specialists, speech pathologists, reading specialists, and government employees. According to Helen Axel of the Conference Board, a business research group, "more jobs lend themselves [today] to offbeat schedules—project-oriented work, research, computer operations and other service activities."[9] Such jobs pay much better than clerical positions because of the advanced education and experience involved. And, if you work twenty-five hours a week or more you can often get benefits.

Job Sharing. This is another option for professional part-timers and is becoming increasingly sought after by women with children. Job sharing means that two, and occasionally three, employees share one job, dividing the various responsibilities and tasks of that job. Fringe benefits and pay are prorated according to whether duties are divided in half, three quarters/one quarter, or in some other division. Some people consider job sharing a fad. But as Caroline Bird states in the foreword to *Working Free*, "What's alternative today is mainstream tomorrow."[10]

One of the reasons job sharing may become more and more acceptable as time goes on is that once all the benefits and salary divisions have been negotiated, the employer fares as well or *better* than the job sharers. Two employers in Wisconsin describe the improvements in work done by job sharers:

> Not only has the productivity of the department increased, but also the quality of the overall service is rising very quickly. Time is not wasted through simple inactivity or through performance of an it-makes-me-look busy task.

> One positive and quite unexpected spin-off we have noticed is that our office has been forced to re-examine and streamline certain processes and abandon or transfer others. It's possible that this might not have occurred if the job sharers hadn't observed how much time they spend on routine paper shuffling. Apparently one gets a much better view of what constitutes wasted effort from a [in this case] four-hour-per-day perspective.[11]

Employers also benefit because they are getting two employees for the price of one, each employee contributing his or her unique background, education, and expertise. They are also getting two fresh, enthusiastic employees who give 100 percent for the period of time they are on the job. As two job-sharing editors in Massachusetts said, "We're a good deal."

With such advantages, one question to ask is, why don't more employers schedule more job-sharing positions? One answer is that there is some math and paper work to do in figuring out how to divide time, salary, benefits, and duties. Another reason is that some jobs, like high-level managerial positions, are not easily adapted to job sharing. The third reason it isn't more popular is that job sharing *is* new. Employers are often slow to change.

But in spite of some employers' reluctance, job sharing is catching on and is especially popular in California and Hawaii. In thinking about the possibilities of job sharing, it's important to know a few facts. Sixty-five percent of job sharers were already working for their employer when they began sharing, and one half of individual job sharers knew each other before splitting the responsibilities of a position.[12] A woman who has been out of the labor force to raise children has the best chance of finding a good job to share if she is a former long-standing employee at a firm or has a good track record at another, similar company, school, or agency. To find a shared position, you should contact former employers, analyze want ads for full-time jobs that could be split, and advertise for a job sharer through a college alumni/ae newsletter or a professional journal.

Job sharers I spoke with said that the two most important things for initially landing the kind of job they wanted were good communication with their sharer and careful preparation of a job proposal and joint résumé for their present or potential employer (appendix A lists books and organizations that will help you do this). Table 7–1 gives an example of a job-sharing discussion between potential partners, figure 7–1 gives an example of a joint résumé, and table 7–2 outlines a proposal to be presented to an employer.

Table 7–1
Preliminary Discussion between Job-sharing Partners

Are our philosophies compatible and our skills complementary?

Can we communicate well?

What strengths and weaknesses would we bring to the position?

Can we trust each other and follow through on decisions?

Do we operate at the same level of commitment and exert similar amounts of effort?

What do we expect from each other?

How will we schedule our time—how will we overlap our schedules?

Will we be flexible and cover for each in the event of a child's illness or other emergencies?

How do we wish to divide benefits?

What communication method(s) will we use to transfer all necessary information to each other?

How can we best approach problem solving and decision making as a team?

Noting all ongoing yearly, monthly, weekly, and daily responsibilities, how will each be handled? What about new responsibilities?

What about housekeeping: desk, files, equipment, and so forth?

Who is entitled to the position if it is made full-time?

Source: Kathleen Sciarappa, lecture on job sharing, with handouts, YWCA, Manchester, N.H., summer, 1985. Reprinted with permission of the author.

Résumé

Jane Smith	Susan Doe
Address	Address
and	and
Phone number	Phone number

Education:

B.A., Oberlin College, 1973

Certificate from Radcliffe Publishing Procedures Course, 1974

Experience:

Editorial Assistant, Allyn & Bacon, 1974–78

Free-lance copy editor, 1978–83

Editor, *Rockingham Gazette*, 1983 to present

Education:

B.A., University of Missouri, 1972

M.A. in English, Boston University, 1974

Experience:

Public Relations Assistant, Newcastle and Associates, 1974–76

Copywriter, Bale and Sawyer, 1976–79

Editor, *Tides*, 1979–85

Copywriter, Bale and Sawyer, 1985 to present

Summary of Skills:

Writing press releases	Research	Videotape editing
Copywriting	Interviewing	Management
Scriptwriting for TV commercials	Photography	Copyediting
Designing and writing promotional brochures	Layout	Substantive editing

Professional Organizations:

Women's Press Club, college alumni associations, college recruitment committee, American Association of University Women

References and publications furnished upon request

Figure 7-1. A Sample Joint Résumé

Table 7–2
Outline for Proposal to Employer for Job-shared Position

Definition of job sharing

The prevalence of job sharing

Profiles of experienced sharers

The advantages of job sharing

Schedule and proposed work plan:
  weekly schedule
  dual coverage
  conferences
  illness/emergencies
  communication
  referral and feedback
  housekeeping
  philosophies
  relationships with other employees and clients

Benefits, taxes, and social security payments

Specific responsibilities

Accountability

Source: Kathleen Sciarappa, lecture on job sharing, with handouts, YWCA, Manchester, N.H., summer, 1985. Reprinted with permission of the author.

Obviously, you have to do a lot of preliminary work to set up a job sharing arrangement, especially if the employer is conservative and is a stranger to you. But the more work you do writing a proposal—thinking of all possible objections and planning to discuss the many advantages with an employer—the better your chances of landing a well-paying job and enjoying it to the fullest.

Starting Your Own Business. If you have skills and experience in a particular area and don't want to work for someone else, you might be interested in starting your own small business. The most prudent way to begin a business without a huge outlay of capital is to start at home, later expanding to an outside location. But if this sounds undesirable, consider a franchise or a business with a former business associate. Be sure to get professional advice from the start. Contact consultants, like AWED (the American Women's Economic Development Corporation) or SCORE (Service Corps of Retired Executives), which are listed in the appendix of this book. Or get advice free of charge from your local chamber of commerce, small business administration office, Internal Revenue Service, or business network. Spend a few hours with a lawyer and an accountant and talk to others who are in business for themselves. For a full-scale business outside the home, at least a hundred hours of study and legwork will be needed before you even talk to a realtor about renting space (for a discussion of smaller-scale part-time businesses that can be adapted to working at home, see chapter 8).

In deciding what exactly you will do and where and when, consider your children. If your child/children are in school every day till 2:30 or if you're married and plan to work at night, then child care is no problem. At most, you might have to ask a neighbor or high school sitter come in when you have an occasional conflict. But if this is not your situation, your children may have a lot of influence on your choice of work.

Part-Time Work and Caring for Children

Although it is unusual for a single mother to survive financially with part-time work, it has been done. It helps if you have only one or two children and some savings, dependable child support, and close friends and relatives willing to help out occasionally. One single parent who did not want her child in a daytime baby-sitting situation had a neighborhood teenage sitter who could care for her daughter in the evenings, and an ex-husband who wanted to spend time with his child every weekend. This woman's skills were wallpapering and painting, and singing. Her most productive time of the day was evening. So she freelanced, setting up gigs for the weekend with a fellow entertainer, and doing commercial wallpapering for restaurants and office buildings weekday evenings after her child was asleep. Another single mother found that a combination of evening teaching jobs and at-home work was an improvement for her over what she at first thought would be ideal: hours at her long-time, "pre-baby" job arranged on a flex-time schedule. "Ironically, it has taken all my feminism and activism to find the place where I can parent and be content . . . that place is home."[13]

Flexibility is important, especially when you have the privilege to set your own hours. A young Nebraska mother writing to the newsletter *New Beginnings* described her experience bringing her children to the small clothing store she owned. She set up an area away from the main activity of the store with a crib and a playpen. Sometimes she had her son in an infant seat on the counter or sat with him in a rocker. With the help of a part-time sales-person, she was able to talk with sales reps, help customers, and do the general business of the store. Her child obligingly napped a great deal, which meant late nights for him, but also more time with his father. All this worked "wonderfully" for two years, but things changed with the birth of a second child who was "fussy and very demanding." At that point her two-year-old was "feeling cramped in the store" and needed to be outside playing. So she sold the store to stay home for a few years with her children and pursued an advanced degree.[14]

For many of us in such a situation this would be a healthy decision. Every child is different and every child changes constantly. The only thing you can really count on is that they'll grow up faster than you can believe. If things that worked well at one stage in a child's development don't continue to, you have to make changes. The highest rate of job satisfaction for working mothers is among part-timers, but choosing part-time work outside the home is no guarantee that things will turn out perfectly. As one job sharer said, "It's often a trade-off. You can't get the ideal situation all the time with everybody in the family. You simply try to set up the best possible situation for your child's care for the hours you're not home."

One option that many part-timers choose for their children is a few hours of day care while they are working. Although day care centers and family day care homes cater to families needing full-time care, there are facilities that will take children part-time. An even more popular option for parents with children over the age of three is nursery school. Nursery schools have excellent morning programs and sometimes extended afternoon hours, too. Neighbors, relatives, and friends who don't feel that they can make a full-time commitment to baby-sitting are sometimes happy to sit on a permanent part-time basis. If you work in the afternoons, you could consider having a high school student come in to sit. Some high schools have baby-sitting courses that include instruction in first aid and simple cooking. Three of the best people who have cared for my children on a part-time basis have been responsible fourteen-year-olds.

Disadvantages of Part-Time Work
Outside the Home

In almost any type of part-time work outside the home, there are some disadvantages. Women in conventional part-time office or retail jobs where they are in the public eye have to spend as much money on clothes as women working full-time. Anyone who works half-days but every day has the same commuting expenses as her full-time colleagues. Women in part-time jobs that aren't professional or semiprofessional sometimes find that the pay is "not worth leaving home for." In short, for some mothers, there can be all the expenses and disadvantages of full-time work without the advantages of full-time pay. Because of these disadvantages, many women who must make money for their families, turn to work at home.

8

Making Money at Home, Nap Time, Nighttime, Anytime You Can

A MOTHER making money at home is following an old tradition of American women. Women in both colonial and independent America ran boarding houses and inns; kept books for businesses; made and sold cheese and other foodstuffs; and assisted in operating farms, dairies, and various small businesses. Most women also manufactured many goods for home consumption. In fact, in the 1770s, one way of thwarting the British and evading their taxes was for women to make their own items like candles, soaps, and clothing. The British government preferred that the colonists sell raw materials to the British, who would manufacture goods from them to be sold back to the colonists. "Making your own" was an effective method of boycotting such British household goods and was an expression of independence. In general, women enjoyed greater independence and fewer social restrictions in the early United States and Canada than in England and Europe.

Today there are virtually no restrictions and therefore no limits to what women can do to earn a living. Millions of women who want or must work at home are finding a wonderful variety of ways to do so. Here is a list of only a few of the possibilities:

Gourmet caterer

Manager of bed and breakfast inn

Seamstress/dress designer

Writer/editor

Designer of computer software

Typing/word-processor businesswoman

Accountant

Direct sales representative

Psychologist

Restaurant owner

Career counselor

Paralegal

All that's really required in devising an appropriate job is an imagination. (For specific examples of women who earn income at home, see appendix B.)

One of the best things about working at home that is cited by women who are doing it is that work can take up only a few hours while children are little, but can later expand to three-quarter or full-time. As one interior designer said, "By working part-time I manage to keep my foot in the door. I can push that door wide open later on in my life, when the time is right."[1]

Assessing Your Children's Needs

As in part-time work outside the home, there are certain assessments that a mother wanting to work at home should make, particularly in regard to children. Ask yourself: Do your children take naps frequently and regularly? Are they active? Loud? Quiet? Dependent? Self-sufficient? Do they like playing outside in the yard and at friends' houses? Do they fight or get along reasonably well with siblings? Is one (or more) able to help with household chores? Do they happily watch TV programs you approve of, or is an older child likely to switch the channel to the kind of videos that would have been X-rated movies when we were in school? And finally, are your children at an age when they can understand that you are a separate person with your own needs and responsibilities?

After asking such questions, you will probably be able to identify some potential problems. As long as you are not looking for an unreasonably large block of time for yourself (and therefore unusually good behavior from your children), you can usually work things out. But it is important to ask the initial questions. Lately there have been many books and magazine articles on entrepreneurial mothers that paint an ideal picture of the woman working at home. It runs something like this: Sylvia Smith, who studied dress designing in Paris, designs and makes exquisite sequined gowns at her home in suburban Chicago (*and* has a seven figure income), while twin two-year-old daughters Susie and Sarah play happily in a corner of her workroom hour after hour. We all know quite well that in fact Susie and Sarah are restless after only an hour of playing dolls and creatively cutting up fabric. They stick pins into each other when they get on each other's nerves, and periodically their mother, Sylvia, screams at them.

It's wise to be realistic. Some of these published entrepreneurial stories are just the flip side of the Supermom record. A great deal of money-earning labor *can* be done at home and millions of women prove this every day. But, depending on the ages and personalities of your children, the work will probably not be steady for any more than a couple of hours at a time. Even now, when my children are in school, I find that the income-producing work I do is woven under and over and around breakfast, laundry, math drills, errands, dinner, and bedtime. Here is what I think is a realistic view of how much work you can hope to get done according to the age of your youngest child:

Baby, birth to 4 months..........Zero work; enjoy the baby and rest

Baby, 4 to 18 months..............2–3 hours a day

Child, 18 months–3 years.......2–4 hours a day

Child, 3–5 years....................2–4 hours a day, sometimes more

School-age child.....................5–8 hours a day

With this in mind, it is often a good idea to set up a schedule that you alter as your children grow and change. The key word to working happily at home with small children is the word "manageability." It's important to avoid taking on too much. During the fleeting years before children go off to school, I think the goal should be to help pay the rent while enjoying them. If you find that your goals for income-producing work are not manageable, when your child is a terrible two-year old, for example, cut back for awhile.

Assessing Your Own Capabilities and Interests

As far as your capabilities for at-home work are concerned, it is good to ask yourself some of the same questions that are asked in chapters 6 and 7. For example, when is your "prime time?" Are you a self-starter? Well disciplined? Easily distracted? Are you reasonably well organized? Even if the answer to some of these last questions is no, it's all right. It just indicates where you need to make some changes—or it may mean that you'd be better off getting a part-time job outside the home.

According to Georganne Fiumara, the organizer of Mothers' Home Business Network, the most important personal attributes you must have to succeed in at-home work are "a willingness to work hard, build a positive self-image, believe in your abilities, build relationships with others who can help you advance your goals and know who your customers are and fulfill their needs."[2] The general dictum "to sell your product, sell yourself" applies to success in an at-home business just as it does for any other business.

One of the most thorough "tests" to determine whether working at home is right for you is the "Suitability Survey" in the book *Working from Home*. The authors also provide a great deal of information on the range of at-home opportunities and details about taxes, zoning, and operating expenses. See appendix A for other books and check your own public library and local bookstore. Find out, too, whether there are workshops or classes at local colleges and vocational or technical schools, adult education classes, small business administration seminars, lectures at the local chamber of commerce, and courses given by the IRS or private firms on small businesses.

The most important consideration in all of this is, of course, what exactly you're going to do. Entrepreneur David Birch of Cambridge, Massachusetts, stresses the need to find something you enjoy. "If you're in it [only] for the money, it just won't work. It should flow out of something you really enjoy." Most experts suggest that you list all the things you've ever done on a piece of paper—athletics, jobs, hobbies, interests, travel—no matter what your level of experience in each. The list should include activities and tasks you weren't paid for. It's then best to analyze what exactly you liked about each. This should help you to determine what you're going to do.

Basically, at-home employment falls into two categories: providing a service or providing a product, such as crafts. Within these two areas, there are thousands and thousands of possibilities.

Providing a Service

Examples of a service include landscaping, legal counsel, accounting, or word processing. Many women provide a service using skills they learned when they were working full-time that they can easily adapt to a home working situation. But often, the service that these women can offer their community has grown out of an interest that began while they were at home, like doing children's portraits or kitchen renovations. These kinds of services frequently offer the best opportunity for professional growing while you are at home with children and can be expanded as the children get older. Generally, they give you the best opportunity for making money.

Day Care. A significant part of service opportunities are found in what are called social services or human services. One of the most common for women at home is day care because it's such a good way to combine caring for your own children while making some money at home. But I strongly urge anyone who is interested in day care to regard it as an important *profession.* If you have no background in child care or teaching, take a couple of courses in areas like child development and creative play. If you cannot afford to do this, read as many books, magazines, and journals as you can find. It is true that the most important qualification for being a good day care provider is love and respect for small children. But it is also true that the job of caring for several preschoolers close in age is an awesome one. So you need as much guidance as you can get.

Join a Family Day Care Association if there is one in your area, and if there is not, contact the state agency that oversees child care and make contact with other mothers on their child care list. But one way or another, find a way to network with other day care providers so that you have people to exchange information with and to work with in joint activities and field trips. Day care is very hard work and therefore it has a high turnover rate. You will be less likely to join the turnover statistics if you can minimize your sense of isolation and increase your enjoyment of the job.

Direct Sales. Another common type of at-home service job is representing a direct sales company. Though you sell a product, you don't produce it yourself. Rather, you make it easy for customers to buy a product, usually in their homes. Two of the best-known direct sales companies are Tupperware and Mary Kay Cosmetics. These companies sell directly to their customers through you and therefore avoid the expense of distributors and all kinds of middlemen. They therefore make quite a profit. The question for you then is: will you? With most of these companies you initially have to invest your own money, though admittedly, it is usually not much. Generally, in order to make several thousand dollars a year, you have to build a network of other women in your region, getting a share of their profits because you've brought them into the system as well as your own profits.

If you like selling, direct sales might be for you. One of the biggest advantages of direct sales is that solid marketing ideas for the product are devised by professionals at the company's headquarters. So you are not alone and ignorant about your methods of reaching customers. It's a good way to start out, to learn about marketing and how to project yourself effectively.

One objection to direct sales is that some of the market strategies that are devised at headquarters involve conducting parties in your home, complete with silly hats and sillier games. If this turns you off but the product doesn't, find out if these parties can be modified or dispensed with. Another objection is that the products themselves are geared to the domestic scene or to the makeup mirror. The number of exceptions, however, is increasing. A young mother from Manitoba, Canada, wrote to tell me about a line of children's music that she feels very good about promoting and selling. There are also books and other educational materials that you can sell. For information on a direct sales company that you might like to work with, contact the Direct Sales Association in Washington, D.C. Check out the reputation of any company that is not a member of DSA with the local Better Business Bureau.

Mail-Order. One of the advantages of direct selling is that you do paperwork at home but get out of the house to do the actual selling. But if you would rather spend most of your time at home, consider starting a mail-order business. Read the stories of other people who've done this successfully in *Inc.* magazine and other entrepreneurial and business magazines. In mail-order, you are both creating a product and providing a service to customers who enjoy the convenience of ordering things from their home. Most mail-order businesses are thriving right now, but be sure that you learn all the details of the business before beginning.

Producing a Product: Crafts

Handcrafts lend themselves well to mail-order as well as to other types of selling, particularly if they are lightweight so that the customer does not have to pay much in postage. If you have skills in a handcraft, you might want to take advantage of the interest today in high quality in general and handcrafted quality in particular. Making and selling handmade items is one of the most creatively satisfying ways to make money at home.

But there are some things to watch out for, according to two experienced craftspeople I talked with. There is often a lot of repetition. One said: "You may like making one pot holder with an appliquéd pineapple, but will you want to make ten in one weekend?" There is also considerable pressure right before Christmas and summer craft shows. And "a woman has to decide if she wants to have her favorite hobby turn into a business with all that that entails." Another word of caution: profit margins are often slim. One woman I interviewed was enormously talented in handcrafts, but said that they weren't worth doing as a business because her supplies were so expensive.

Buying Supplies, and Other Expenses. So, before you begin a craft business, find out the best and least expensive way to buy supplies, preferably wholesale. Be sure to buy the best possible materials. For most potential customers, the whole point in buying handcrafted items rather than mass-produced is the quality. If the materials you use are obviously good, you can sell items for more. One craftswoman found that if she sold small, quilted squares as wallhanging "folk art," rather than making the intricate squares into pillows or pot holders, she could charge what her time and thought and detailed handwork were worth. Remember that the labor you expend making something is the same whether materials are cheap or very good. Your labor is important, and it's unwise to waste it on something that may wind up looking shoddy. If you're going to go crosseyed at 2:00 A.M. before a big craft show, you might as well get the best possible price for your time and effort the next day.

In addition to basic supplies, there are other expenses involved, particularly if you sell your crafts through craft shows. You must buy space, pay for transportation, food, collapsible display tables, and signs. This outlay of cash means that some women make no profit their first year of business. But for many, it's worth it. According to one couple who initially sold at craft fairs only,

> You get to know other craftspeople and see what they're doing. You learn a lot about the business end of the business: wholesalers, shows coming up, marketing devices, attractive display techniques, and how to generate a mailing list. You also learn what the basic response of the public is to the items you are selling. You can tell when one of the things you think is clever is a real bomb to the public.

Marketing Representatives. For mothers who don't like the idea of being away from home on a weekend or don't want to pay the fees involved in craft fairs, there is an alternative: marketing representatives. Marketing reps are go-betweens for the craftsperson and the marketplace, especially gift shops. Initially no expenditure of money is required on your part. You sign a contract with a rep to market and sell your craft items. He or she peddles your goods to gift shops or in another appropriate market nationally. You get an order from the rep, mail out the order to the shop, and pay 10–20 percent of the order to the rep within thirty days. If the rep can't sell your stuff, you are free to get out of the contract by giving written notice to that effect within thirty days; the rep has the same right.

The only disadvantage to marketing reps is that they are sometimes very hard to find. Your best bet is with someone who is new in the business and eager to get new clients. To find out where a regional trade mart is (and the offices of marketing reps), call local gift shops and stores and ask them where the local mart is located, or look in the yellow pages under "Gifts, wholesale." You can also go to a regional gift show, buy a catalogue, and look up the names and addresses of the marketing representatives listed (see appendix A for the names of two of the largest regional trade marts).

You can, of course, sell your crafts yourself at local stores. You can also sell crafts from your home if this appeals to you and the zoning laws allow it.

Diversifying and Expanding. Some women have made a financial success of crafts by diversifying and slowly expanding. Two quilters I talked with who started out selling large and small quilted items at local craft fairs also took orders for custom-made quilts. Their custom-order business slowly expanded, and later, when their children were all in school, they opened a quilt shop selling their own and fellow quilters' things, fabrics and notions, stenciling materials, craft books, and patterns. They also taught classes in quilting and later hired additional teachers and salespeople in order to expand further.

Craftswoman Constance Hallinan Lagan of North Babylon, New York, teaches crafts at her home, writes articles for crafts magazines, lectures widely, produces attractive how-to manuals for craftspeople called "Marketing Options Reports," and hires herself out as a consultant. She is extremely professional in all her endeavors and urges other craftspeople to register their businesses' names, collect sales tax, and consult with the IRS in order to be as businesslike as possible.

Crafts Co-ops. If this and other aspects of creating and running a crafts business sound like more time and work than you want to invest, you might consider joining a crafts co-op. If there are any in the area where you live, your state or county craft league should have a list. If there aren't any nearby, you might consider starting a co-op with friends. The basic rules for starting a crafts co-op are the same as those for a food or baby-sitting co-op. In fact, some craft co-ops may resemble a baby-sitting co-op in that a corner of the craft co-op's shop or work area is often set up for little children to play in while their mothers work.

Cottage Industries

An enterprise similar to co-oping is an at-home business run by one individual that becomes so successful that she has to hire outside help. It then becomes what is known as a cottage industry. An example is The Silent Woman, a small sewing business headed by a Ripon, Wisconsin, housewife, Jean Bice. Mrs. Bice provides the women who work for her with notions, fabric, and a picture of the garment they are to make. Most of her employees earn about $8,000 a year.[3]

One of the most successful and long-running cottage industries in this country is that of the home knitters of New England who make items on knitting machines in their homes. Many of these women work for a manufacturer who is willing to let them work at home rather than at the factory. Though some of these women make as much as $15,000 a year, they as well as Mrs. Bice and her employees have been under fire recently. Labor unions have accused companies of violating a forty-year-old federal regulation that prohibits home workers in the knitting industry. The regulation was originally enacted to protect immigrants from being exploited, and because home workers usually get no pension or health insurance benefits, the International Ladies Garment Workers' Union has tried to have this regulation reinstated since it was overturned by the Reagan Administration in 1981. The ILGWU has insisted that "the typical woman . . . is in the barrio or slum of a major city, she is a minority or a poor white, she is an undocumented worker and she is grossly underpaid."[4] The home knitters and their employers, sometimes knitters themselves, of course, have insisted that this is rubbish, and the debate goes on, with the ban on home knitting periodically lifted and then reinforced.[5] At this time, knitters and seamstresses are legally allowed to do their work at home.

"Electronic Cottagers"

Actually, the debate has had far-reaching effects because it also involves a growing group of both men and women who work at home: "electronic cottagers." This term was coined by futurist Alvin Toffler to designate those people who work at home at a company-supplied computer terminal, with a national telephone hook-up, or with their own desk computer. Labor attorneys and union officials have charged that "rather than looking at the cottage industry of the future, we may be looking at an electronic sweatshop, which takes us backwards, rather than forwards."[6] One of the strongest objections of union officials has been that some of the women doing clerical work at computer terminals installed in their homes or taking orders over the telephone for a national retail network are paid less per hour than office workers and have no benefits because they are part-time workers. However, mothers at home doing this kind of work insist that they make the same or more than their office counterparts because they save money on clothes, day care, and commuter costs. Most of them are married and have health insurance through their husbands. They are enthusiastic about being "electronic cottagers."

If you have a long track record with a large company that is in the vanguard of the electronic cottage movement, you might be able to get a job working part-time at home. Generally, companies will not install expensive telecommunications equipment in a home unless the employee is well known or well recommended.

However, another group of electronic cottagers may far outnumber the group of clerical workers at home with a terminal. I found that a surprising number of women are starting word-processing businesses at home after being successful with a typing business. There are also other jobs that can be done with a desk computer: Keeping other businesses' accounts and orders straight for them, designing software, and writing software instruction manuals. In addition, there is a growing need to teach adults how to use a computer, and women who teach these courses do much of their preparatory work on a home computer. Newspaper reporters covering a particular region for a major newspaper use word processors to write their stories and then "send them in" through a computer terminal installed by their newspaper. So the number of professions that can be adapted to electronic home work is growing.

Financing Your Home Business

If you need to get financing in order to buy something like a computer or expand a business when your children get older, you should take a how-to-get-financing seminar at your local chamber of commerce or small business organization. It's also a good idea to read magazines like *Inc.* and *Money* to get tips. If you cannot find financing after going to several banks, consider contacting a venture capitalist. This is someone with "disposable income" who likes investing in small, promising companies instead of more conventional businesses. He or she is usually most interested in successful ventures that are expanding because their market is increasing. To find a willing capitalist, contact the Venture Capital Network in your area or contact professional advisors like the Entrepreneurial Institute (see appendix A).

On the other hand, if your business is nonprofit, like a health care service or a children's museum, you might look into applying for a grant from an appropriate organization. Also, look into the Small Business Administration's guaranteed loan program, which, as of this writing, is still in existence. This program guarantees up to 90 percent or more of a bank loan, so it is a help to companies that, without the guarantee, would be turned down by banks.[7]

I recommend that women planning to work at home avoid borrowing money either privately or from a bank. Women constitute the fastest growing group of entrepreneurs in the United States, but more businesses fail than succeed. So start out thinking small.

If you have to borrow, be sure to have a solid business proposal to show your potential lender. The proposal should be based on a business plan, which is something everyone should have whether starting out big or small. In a business plan, you identify potential customers; determine how you will reach them; decide on a monthly budget and collection procedures; determine where you will buy raw materials; decide how to package and deliver your product if that's relevant; and consider whether you'll need to hire seasonal or occasional help. It may seem ridiculous to write down things like this if you're planning something small in scope, but it's a good idea to force yourself to do it. As one writer put it, "Refusal to commit your plans to paper may reflect an unwillingness to face potential problems involved with any new business venture or may be a way of fooling yourself into believing that problems do not exist."[8]

No matter how modest an enterprise you start, you will face some basic expenses in getting the word out about your service or product. In some businesses—such as child care—demand is such that all you need to do is put an ad in the paper for a few dollars and your phone will be ringing off the hook. But in a good many part-time, at-home businesses, marketing and advertising are important, and there are some important steps to take. First, think about your potential customers. Be calculating enough to consider what income group you will appeal to. If you appeal to a general middle-income group you will sell more, but will probably have to charge less for your product or service. With a higher-income market, the reverse is usually true.

Your Potential Customer

Ask yourself how the product or service you want to provide will benefit your customer. What would he or she be most interested in, and what are you best qualified to provide: Low price? Special service? Attention to detail? Accessibility? What do you know about your customer's life-style and spending inclinations? You have to focus all your efforts directly on this potential customer. Then be sure to compare your product or service with that of the competition. List your competitors' products and their prices and special services. How will you be different from your competition?

It may seem that these are awfully serious questions to be asking yourself. I think at first the natural tendency is to say "But I'm just going to be selling my homemade banana bread at sports events on Saturday afternoons." The fact remains that you will put a lot of time, effort, and thought into baking and selling the bread. There is nothing sadder than high hopes and wasted effort. I spoke to a young mother with two preschoolers who spent two weeks making quilted handcrafts, paid fifty dollars for a booth at a craft fair, spent several dollars on gas to get there, spent ten hours of her day at the fair, and *sold nothing.* The reason she did so poorly was that the craft fair was crammed with quilted handcrafts.

If you can see realistically that your product or service could meet the same fate in the market you are considering, don't become discouraged. You may simply be looking in the wrong place where the competition is too stiff. One crafts couple I spoke to in Maine had difficulty selling their New England crafts to New Englanders in the three-state area they first targeted, but did a fantastic business in the West and Southwest through national market representatives. So be flexible enough to work around the problems of competition.

The Value of Networking

Many mothers operating a small venture from home find that it's possible to avoid the negative aspects of competition by networking. This approach works particularly well for businesses that provide services like accounting, word processing, public relations, legal advice, or psychotherapy. The national networks for women working at home are the Mothers' Home Business Network and National Alliance of Home-based Businesswomen (see appendix A), but there are also state and local networks in many areas, as well as guilds, clubs, and other organizations that can provide a network of referrals and information. Use your phone book, local library, community center, or chamber of commerce to find an appropriate network.

Apart from making life more pleasant and profitable, networking can also help you make friends who can help in a pinch. If you are ever overwhelmed with business but hate to turn away a customer completely, you can call on someone in your field to do the extra work. While there is always the risk of losing a customer this way, women who network say that they give customers better service this way because one way or another the customer gets what he or she needs. Women also get as many referrals as they give. According to a word-processing entrepreneur, it's best to "try cooperation instead of competition."[9]

Other Considerations: Overhead, Office Hours, and Scope

If you will need to buy raw materials and supplies, be certain to look at your local community in terms of how readily available and/or expensive supplies are. Overhead expenses can have an enormous impact on profits. If you want to put up a sign for your business, find out what zoning regulations are in force where you live and what is involved in getting a variance. Think also about whether or not you want to have clients/customers coming to your house, and "seeing your two-year-old's Dr. Denton's draped over a chair or peanut butter smeared on the kitchen counter," as one mother put it. For many of us, part of the point of working at home is for the privilege of cleaning the house later and working half the morning in a bathrobe if we feel like it. But if you need or want to have people coming to your house, think about maintaining specific office hours.

Another general area to think about is scope: How big is your business going to be? Will you stick to one community, or reach out to others through advertising and mail-order? Do you want from the beginning to plan on gradual expansion, or do you prefer simply to start small and see what happens? Do you want to stay home to do all your work, or have a combination: some at home, some at the customer's place of business, and some "on the road"?

Getting the Word Out

No matter what the scope or sphere of activity of your business, you should have a business card. If you want a really super-looking card with a logo (a symbol representing your business), you can have a card designed professionally. But it's also quite satisfactory to select lettering from a catalogue at a photocopier like pip (postal instant press) and have cards made up for you. This is definitely the most inexpensive way to get cards (about $20.00 for

500) and is adequate for those of us who have a nofrills kind of business. In deciding what exactly to have printed on your cards, be sure to be very specific about what you are offering. If you are too vague, you may wind up with a lot of phone calls from people you can't help, and telling them so means a lot of work time lost. The most important thing about business cards is to *get rid of them:* give them to people every chance you get, put them up on appropriate bulletin boards, and, if you can find someone willing, leave a stack of them in a dispenser at a related business.

The same rule applies to brochures and folders. If you go to the trouble of writing them and having them printed up, *get them out, give them away.* Folders, by the way, can be inexpensively produced by writing about your business on a folded legal-sized piece of paper, having it photocopied on colored paper, and folding and mailing it yourself. Mailing lists can be bought, but you can also make them up yourself by consulting the phone book or trade lists, and by getting referrals.

If you think that you want to do more to advertise your service or product, look into methods that are free. For example, many local newspapers have a "new businesses in town" section. A reporter may interview you in person or on the phone and then write a sizeable description of you and your venture. Often the paper will take a picture, too. There are other local publications like shoppers' flyers, regional magazines, and business digests that also list or do articles on new businesses. You yourself can also write about your business by doing press releases for local newspapers when you first start working at home. Whenever you have the slightest change in your business—an improved product, a new service, or a person to assist you— you can write another press release. There are many, many other ways to advertise what you are doing. Appendix A lists a helpful guide.

Establishing Your Professionalism

Most women working at home part- or full-time suggest that you devise a name for your business. It's a good idea to register that name with your state's secretary of state in order to protect yourself from having your business's name duplicated. If someone else is already using the name, the state office will let you know, which can save you confusion and legal hassles. It may also be a good idea to fill out an Internal Revenue Service form for an Employer Identification number, which the IRS will send you free after receiving the form. The advantage to an EI number is that it enables you to look more professional to the IRS and minimizes the chances of your having any problems with it.

In the past, some have criticized men and women working at home, assuming that they do not declare income and therefore get out of paying income taxes. Some of this criticism is valid. However, one trend among women with at-home businesses is an effort to be professional, declaring all profits, paying federal and state taxes, *and* getting all the allowable deductions when tax time rolls around. All the books, articles, entrepreneurial newsletters, and small business consultants point out that there are many professional and financial benefits to "doing it the right way." Making out all the necessary state and federal forms and paying required sales taxes legitimizes the at-home worker's endeavors and can have some nice results in lowering personal taxes.

Setting Up a Work Space at Home

If you want to take your work space as a deduction, you can as long as the area is used *exclusively* for your business. Many people think that if you use only part of a room you cannot take a deduction. But in some cases, this is okay. You can delineate a third of a large room, for example, and as long as this area is used only for your business, it will be accepted for deduction.

Apart from any concern with the Internal Revenue Service, it is important to have a space that is used only for your work. Some people can simply use the kitchen table and clear it up at the end of the day with no problems. But most of us are not this well organized or clean. If finding "your own space" is difficult, make a list of possible work areas: an enclosed porch, an attic, cellar, entryway, storage closet, or hallway corner. If none of these places yields space, consider using one end of a reasonably large room like the living room or master bedroom. You can define this area by placing a desk or a wide bookcase across the width of the room. The space between the end of the desk or bookcase and the other wall is the "door" to your workroom. You can hang planters or decorative objects above the desk or bookcase to create the illusion of a "wall."

Once you have a specific work area you will need to furnish it, perhaps with secondhand furniture or your own furniture adapted to your needs. You can buy metal or cardboard filing cabinets if you need them or simply get cardboard liquor boxes the size of file folders. However you set up your space, make it efficient and pleasant and be sure everyone understands that it is *yours.*

In organizing your work space, consider whether you will be working during hours other than nap time, evenings, or school hours, that is, times when your children are not occupied. If you will be working at least part of that time, you should position your desk or work table so that the children can see you from the room where they play; or use a playpen in the area where you are working, or set up a "childrens' corner" near you with small toys and books and maybe a beanbag chair to rest in. Once children get to be four or five, it is usually enough that you be close enough for reassurance and talk now and then.

Children and Your At-Home Business

It's a good idea to write out a work schedule for yourself and read it to pre-schoolers. You can then display it in a prominent place for older members of the family to see. Most women I talked to and corresponded with felt that children handle the idea of an at-home working mom pretty well as long as they know when they can count on a mother's full attention. Most women find that it's best to spend an hour or more in the morning doing something exclusively with the children and then getting them busy with something they can do unassisted. Initially, be very firm about the time you need for work. Explain the reasons you are working at home and how your child can contribute by doing his or her own "work" while you do yours. This is not stifling children, and it does not mean that they are in the same position as a child whose mother works full-time outside the home. You are teaching your child responsibility and consideration and *reality.*

But if there is a big problem or you find that your business takes more time than you had expected, consider joining a baby-sitting co-op or play school. When it's your turn to baby-sit, if you schedule your time when you would ordinarily be playing with your own child, your basic work schedule will not be disrupted.

If you can afford it, there is also the option of taking your children to a private nursery school or a day care center. One mother who made catheter bags for hospitals on fairly large equipment in her home found that her children, whom she had adopted in fairly rapid succession, were happier—and she was too—when they were in a day care center across the street from their house. When they were sick or when there was an emergency, she still had the freedom to have the children home with her. As with anything, you have to be flexible and work out whatever is most comfortable for everyone in the family.

By the age of three or so, most children can become actively involved in some aspects of an at-home business, like stuffing envelopes or sorting fabrics. One of the many benefits people working at home cite is that children learn what is involved in putting food on the table: "It's important that they see how work is done. For most kids, work is a place parents go away to, not something they understand.''[10]

Children can help a mother working at home by simply doing chores. For very young children it helps to break down chores into mini–tasks. Don't underestimate how much your child can do, but if he or she shows obvious stress, alter the way you instruct the child to do the work or have him or her do only a manageable portion of the job. There is nothing exploitive about having children be responsible for a number of chores, especially if they are school aged. As an at-home newspaper publisher in South Dakota put it, ''A few chores each day gives them something to do, makes them feel part of the whole plan, and lessens the workload for parents.''[11] Two of the most common problems cited by teenagers with drug problems and by those who try to commit suicide are feeling little self-worth and experiencing malaise. Children with work to do at home that a parent really *needs* them to do don't have much opportunity to have these problems.

To reward them for their part in helping Mom to get an order out or to do important chores, some mothers give their children a small portion of the money they earn in their own ''pay envelope.'' Computer consultant Cynthia Harriman sometimes gives her children five dollars out of a free-lance paycheck: ''But it doesn't necessarily have to be five dollars. A giant cookie at the bakery en route to the bank to deposit my check can work just as well. The point is that this is their share of Mom's pay for the work they did to help her.''

Harriman addresses still another issue that is important to those of us who feel strongly about women's having a specific occupation and being capable of self-support. ''I feel I'm a good role model for my daughter. She sees me working at home every day. She also sees me when I occasionally have to visit clients dressed in my dress-for-success uniform. With a mother who works at home, both sons and daughters get a good sense of the value of both work and family.''[12]

Taking Care of Your Future

Some people express concern that mothers working at home cannot have Social Security exemptions set aside for them. Given the poor return on investment of Social Security and its uncertain future, however, women working at home would be wise to make their own financial plans. In order to set aside money for retirement, a Keogh plan or an IRA, or a combination of both is a much better investment. The Keogh is especially attractive because you don't have to be self-employed full-time to qualify, and you can put up to $30,000 or 25 percent of your income from at-home work (whichever is less) into the plan each year. You can arrange for both IRA and Keogh plans at banks or with brokers.[13]

The idea of putting as much as $30,000 a year into a retirement plan may seem rather remote from the modest goal most of us have set for ourselves in our work at home: to contribute a few thousand dollars (or less) to the family coffers each year and to take care of the children. But one entrepreneurial mother warned against what she calls the "Church Bazaar Syndrome": charging too little for work well done. She was referring specifically to beautifully crafted items sold for only a few dollars, but the syndrome can afflict any woman producing an item or providing a service. So be certain to find out the going rate for whatever you are doing, deliver a professional job, and get what you should.

Working at home is not for everyone. You have to be disciplined and well motivated. You have to balance responsibilities to children and work, with children as the main priority, and yet remain professional so that you can bring in a decent amount of money each year. But for those of us who are enthusiastic "worksteaders," the only thing that really makes us unhappy is that some mothers are unable to earn income at home because they feel too financially insecure to take the plunge.

PART I

Nurturing Ourselves and Others

Dare it arrive, the day when weakness ends?
When the insistence is strong, the wish converted?

— Muriel Rukeyser

9

How Many Kids
Can Ron and Nancy Care for
in the White House Basement?

I N the United States today two ironies bear directly on the American family. We have a conservative administration in the White House that claims to be profamily and all for having Mom at home with the kids, but is nonetheless unwilling to do much concretely to help millions of moderate-income families keep Mom at home. A second irony is occurring at the same time: an administration that would like to cut back on welfare payments to the able-bodied has cut the very funds for subsidized day care for the poor that could help single mothers to become or remain self-supporting. The administration at this writing is reluctant even to admit that a shortage of child care facilities exists in the nation along with a need for these funds.[1]

The Reagan administration has introduced some improvements that address the day care issue, including tax incentives to encourage corporations to set up on-site day care centers. The administration's Office of Human Development has issued guidelines for use by states and cities to implement programs for latchkey children. And the right of women to earn money at home has been strengthened by the Justice Department's overturning of the 1947 ban on home knitting and sewing. But other than these developments and the much touted increase in the child care tax credit to an inadequate 30 percent, the Reagan administration has done little to make life easier for families.

But this situation is not peculiar to the president and political party that happen to be in the White House at this writing. Providing help to families needing child care in order for the mother to work, no matter what her income level, has always met with opposition, and with some justification. Politicians and many of their constituents are reluctant to see legislation pass that might encourage young mothers to work outside the home full-time since the effect on the rest of the family is questionable. At the same time, political leaders cannot decide to help mothers who wish to stay at home. Perhaps they are under the mistaken impression that making it tough for mothers to get good day care for their children will prevent them from working. The last decade has not really borne out this assumption. Those of us who feel that we must work will work no matter how unhappy we may be with our child care arrangements.

The principal problem with any assistance to families is, of course, the expense. But the author of *The Day-Care Dilemma*, Marian Blum, summarizes the reasons government must play a larger role:

> Children are entitled to a healthy, secure, consistent, loving, disciplined, warm, caring, nurtured, unpressured infancy and childhood. It is primarily the responsibility of parents to so provide. But, it is the responsibility of the greater society to create structures and policies that enable parents to do so.
>
> Society must rethink its priorities. If children are as important as off-shore oil; if they are as interesting as computers; if they are as vital to the survival of the United States as nuclear missiles; if they are a national treasure equal to the Grand Canyon; then *someone will have to raise them*. And someone—including parents and the larger society—will have to pay for that care.[2]

I do not believe that a nation can prosper when economic and social pressures combine to push mothers into the work force, while at the same time no system exists for providing consistently good care for their children. Mothers and fathers need good, worry-free care for their children while they work, and those parents who wish to provide that care themselves need adequate tax breaks.

Dimensions of the Problem

It's important to remember that the numbers of mothers with infants and preschoolers in the work force in the last decade has climbed steadily, and 80 percent of these women are in nonexecutive, clerical jobs. In surveys, the majority state that they are working for economic reasons,[3] so their working can hardly be attributed to a desire to leave their children for high-powered, ego-enhancing jobs. Thousands of poor women who wish to work in order to raise their standard of living have been unable to do so because there is no space for their children in federally subsidized child care facilities. Since 1981, Title XX (which funded day care for low-income families) and the child care food program have both been cut back. A study the Children's

Defense Fund conducted to determine the effects of these cutbacks in all fifty states found that in 1983 thirty-two states were providing subsidized care to fewer children than they were in 1981; thirty-one states had changed their eligibility standards, cutting out many families previously eligible; nineteen states had increased fees paid by families; twenty-four states had cut back on funds for training for child care workers; and thirty-three had lowered standards for providing child care.

Here is an example of the effects of this change in just one city. In San Antonio, Texas, 27,000 families were eligible for subsidized child care, according to the 1970 census. A year after the cutbacks of the Reagan administration in 1982, there were only 1,609 day care spaces available for them. According to a report by the San Antonio Coalition for Children, Youth, and Families, some of these children are left during the time their parents are working "in a variety of situations—with relatives, neighbors, older siblings, and in startling and ever-increasing numbers, are left at home alone, with no supervision whatsoever!"⁴ So, although President Reagan promised a profamily administration, that administration has not promoted traditional tax breaks to American women who wish to stay home, nor has it helped provide anxiety-free care for the children of those who work full-time outside the home.

The Administration's Response

President Reagan's facile solution to the day care crisis? "Working mothers [could] drop their kids off at the church, and there are these volunteers to take care of them, and there would be no government involved."⁵ The White House has had an appalling lack of understanding about a problem of huge proportions. The idea that millions of children should be cared for by mostly middle-aged and elderly volunteers eight to nine hours a day, five days a week, twelve months of the year in church basements across the nation would be laughable if it weren't so sad. In responding to the church basement comment, Marian Blum points out that the president ignores the fact that the mothers and grandmothers he designates as the perfect child care volunteers simply because they were once mothers themselves,

> were raising children in small numbers, not in large groups. They had an age range of infants and toddlers and older children. And, they had biological limits to the numbers they dealt with. . . . An analogy ought to be made to the president that mothers and grandmothers have also been cooking and baking for generations. Therefore, the White House ought to make do with a volunteer chef.⁶

The Legislative Response

While the attitudes prevalent in the executive branch have been disappointing to those interested in children's well being, the response of the legislative branch for years has been to gather information but legislate very little. In an attempt to provide an accurate picture for lawmakers and for the public of what families are experiencing in the mid-1980s, the House of Representatives' Select Committee on Children, Youth, and Families has held hearings in Washington, D.C., and in other major U.S. cities. Members have heard testimony about child care outside the home from psychiatrists, child development experts, child care directors, authorities on child care in other countries, home family day care providers, working mothers, community workers, day care center directors, and children themselves who are enrolled in preschool and after-school programs.

Though one of its greatest concerns has been how the federal government can improve day care for the children of working parents, the committee has also been concerned about women who choose to stay at home caring for their children and are having a hard time doing so.

Various groups of mothers at home have written to and testified before the Select Committee. These communications have urged Congress to pass legislation to provide economic and social incentives for mothers who wish to remain at home. These letters have expressed special concern for the

borderline working mother who works not because it puts food on the table, but because her paycheck keeps the family from worrying about unexpected expenses and heightens their lifestyle. Often the husband is pressuring this mother to contribute financially to the family when she would prefer to stay at home with her children and believes in the importance of it. It is this borderline working mother and her husband who might be swung over to staying at home . . . if there were financial incentives . . . that would make staying at home more attractive.

. . . Social incentives that make a statement that mothers at home are a valuable natural resource and that they deserve recognition will begin the turnaround in society's thinking that casts mothers at home as less valuable citizens.[7]

The following are some of the specific recommendations that have been made to help bring this change about:

Incentives to private corporations to offer flex-time, job sharing, and occupations scheduled on "mother-time" (during school hours)

Government leadership in acknowledging skills in management acquired as a homemaker and mother to be listed on résumés when women reenter the work force

A standardized figure representing the "equivalent salary" of a housewife were she working to be published by the federal government (Dome's Home Budget Book has estimated this figure at $36,348 a year)

Income tax deductions for unpaid volunteer contributions of time and expertise to public schools

Flexible labor laws that do not penalize women who wish to have at-home businesses

Equal IRA and social security deposits for homemakers and special mortgages and loans for families with a mother at home (this is part of what has been called the Housewife's Bill of Rights)

Increasing the dependent tax exemption[8]

Advocates for women wishing to remain at home with their infants and other young children stressed that not all of these ideas could be implemented, but that putting any one of them into action would help ease the burden for those families with a mother at home and a small income. They expressed concern that even women at home who wish to contribute economically to their families are sometimes thwarted by restrictive tax provisions and labor laws. The chairman of the committee, Rep. George Miller, recognized after hearing testimony that "the current U.S. income policy is slanted against individuals staying at home."[9] There is some possibility of legislation's being passed to assist at-home mothers.

Republican members of the Select Committee have stated their concern that full-time, wide-scale, institutional care may not be advisable for the infants and young children themselves:

It will be argued that experts have shown that interruption of the mother–infant bond will not cause serious permanent harm to children. But for as many experts as we may find on one side of this question, it will be possible to find others who assert the opposite. . . .

By presenting these thoughts for the consideration of the Committee, we do not intend to say that the government assistance for child care ought to be excluded. Clearly, it cannot be excluded because, although it is not a perfect solution to our problems, it does offer a necessary measure of relief to many persons in great need. Quite simply, we are expressing our inability to be sanguine about a solution for the children of others which we would not want to choose for our own children. Further, we are pointing out that we believe an injustice is done to both children and parents when we omit discussion of the drawbacks of professional child care, when we encourage those who do not absolutely need professional child care to seek it (as is done with the current child care credit available to persons of all income levels), and especially, when we offer assistance to parents only when they choose to place their children in professional care.

. . . Let us consider the situation of a low-income family of four, with two parents and two pre-school children, scraping together on the husband's earnings alone. The wife has made the decision not to seek employment outside the home, or perhaps she has quit her job, because she believes that the most important thing she can give her children during these crucial years is herself. In order to do this, she and her husband are willing to make plenty of sacrifices. As far as they are concerned, the sacrifices are worth it because their children are worth it.

What will the Federal Government do for this family? Very little, if the wife continues to insist upon raising her own children. However, if she will only give up her goal, get a job, and leave her children in the care of someone else for 40 hours a week, she will have not only . . . additional income, but also a subsidy from the government worth about $960 per year.

This situation seems very unfair. Indeed, any proposal which offers assistance to parents and children in need only if the decision is made to place the children in professional care seems both unjust and, as a matter of federal policy, very unwise. Certainly, we ought to be able to devise methods of assistance less coercive than these, by which we might both aid the families and allow them the freedom of choice which is theirs by right.[10]

These members of the committee—Reps. Thomas Bliley, Jr., Frank Wolf, Dan Coats, and Barbara Vucanovich—express sensitivity and fair-mindedness on the issues. In general, all the testimony and discussions at the hearing indicate that the men and women who represent us are concerned with doing the right thing. Unfortunately, the government seldom gets beyond hearings and discussions. Both houses of Congress and both parties seem quite indecisive when it comes to legislation for children.

The Need for a National Policy on Child Care

We need to establish a national policy and national standards for child care to express concern for the nation's children. A national policy would recognize that parents, as long as they are mentally and physically sound, have the right and obligation to choose what they deem best for their children: caring for the children themselves or finding a well-trained care giver. Mothers who are at home caring for their children and struggling financially to stay there have naturally been disturbed that only working mothers may be getting help. So any national policy statement would have to address the concerns of the 50 percent or more of us who are at home with our children full- or part-time.

In view of the different choices individual parents will make, the federal government should not penalize either those who prefer to care for their children themselves or those who choose outside care by subsidizing one group or the other. Nor should it support only one type of day care. It is important to encourage the current variety of choices: private, corporate, church-sponsored, for-profit and nonprofit centers, as well as in-home sitters and family day care. Although I opposed President Nixon's veto of the 1971 Comprehensive Child Development Bill, I now think it was for the best because in addition to the expense, a massive federal program might have led to a standardized, institutionalized approach to care, especially for the poor. Though we now have a hodgepodge of different kinds of care for children that badly needs an umbrella organization for regulation and support, we also have variety, which is not necessarily a bad thing. Thus far, most of the discussion before the Select Committee has focused on funding day care centers and family day care homes.

Tax Reform

One suggestion that could help both families who want good day care and those who want to care for their children themselves is to increase the amount a wage earner can take for exemptions. At other times in its history the U.S. government has supported mother care for children by giving families generous personal and dependent tax exemptions. The personal exemption on income tax, which was introduced in 1913, allows each taxpayer to deduct a certain percentage of his or her income for the expenses of being alive. The dependent exemption, enacted in 1917, allows the taxpayer to deduct a certain amount for each household member. Generally, this was the wife and dependent children of a male breadwinner. The dependent exemptions allowed were largely responsible for maintaining the American custom of having mothers care for babies and young children at home. Until recent years the exemption kept pace with inflation. Now it most certainly does not. It has been estimated by U.S. Treasury official Eugene Steuerle that if the "personal exemption had been indexed for income growth since 1948 . . . then it would equal . . . about $5,600 in 1984."[11]

At the same time, the Social Security tax has steadily climbed. According to Sen. Daniel Patrick Moynihan, "All told, combining Federal income and social security taxes, an American family of median income in 1948 paid about 4.4 percent of its income to the Federal Government. By 1982, the Federal Government was claiming some 18 percent of the median family's income."[12]

What this means to parents in middle-income families is that they either struggle financially so that the mother can stay home or, increasingly, they put together some kind of day care arrangement for the children so the mother can go out to work. In the book *Inequality in an Age of Decline*, Paul Blumberg summarizes what he calls "The New Four-Passenger Treadmill" of the middle-class family:

> The central fact in the postwar rise of the working wife was the desire to boost family income and to offset whatever might have been perceived of the falling rate of affluence among individual workers. . . . Between 1968 and 1978, real gross family income rose only 9 percent, compared to more than 41 percent and 32 percent in the two preceding decades. . . . Inflation has pushed families into higher tax brackets without raising their real income. Because prices doubled between 1967 and 1978, a family that earned $10,000 in 1967 had to earn $20,000 in 1978 just to stay even with inflation. But if a family had doubled its income in this period, it would have moved into a higher federal tax bracket, not to mention the effects of sharply higher Social Security taxes and state and local income taxes. . . . This was partially offset by reductions in the federal income tax over the period for median-income taxpayers. In any case, . . . under the impact of inflation and federal taxes alone, many families were worse off at the end of the 1970s than at the end of the 1960s.[13]

For poor women, particularly those who are the head of a household, things are a great deal tougher, partly because their efforts at work don't result in anything close to a middle-class life-style. The relationship between the cost of raising a family and the amount they are taxed is now "so askew that a poor family . . . is subject to tax. In 1948 the poverty line for a family of four would have been $2,454, or some $200 below the income tax threshold. In 1983 the poverty line was $10,166 for a family of four, but Federal tax liability in that year began at $8,783. . . . The Federal Government was *taxing* the poor at levels without equal in history."[14] What has happened to both middle- and low-income families is that inflation has pushed more families into a tax bracket in which they really do not belong, considering the expenses of providing a family with food, shelter, and other basics.

Though Sen. Moynihan has been accused in the past of making both sexist and racist comments in discussing the plight of poor families headed by women, he argues persuasively today for easing the predicament of all American families caught in the squeeze: "The costs of raising a family no longer bear any relationship to the amount of income not subject to Federal tax."[15] Sen. Moynihan argues that in previous decades the government has chosen not to tax the income required to raise a family and that this was in essence a "powerful national policy." We now have no policy—directly or indirectly—that expresses what our nation regards as important for the health and progress of the American family.

What is now being proposed is indexing the personal and dependent exemptions for inflation, to bring them up to $2,500 per family member. In a family of four, this would mean $10,000. Since many working women— single and married—make about $12,000 a year, this $10,000 would make a significant difference in the lives of millions of American families. Those who work would have many more take-home paycheck dollars with which to buy high-quality child care, and there would be much more competition for child care dollars among providers. Some single mothers who have dependable child support could work part-time instead of full-time. And in two-parent families with an annual income between $15,000 and $25,000, one parent could stay home with young children. There finally could be real choice for American families.

The hitch, of course, is money. It has been estimated that if the dependent and personal exemptions were raised to $2,500 it would cost the federal government $40 billion a year, approximately 10 percent of the revenues now collected from personal income taxes. In the midst of a huge federal deficit, this doesn't sound good to anyone. But once the deficit is brought under control there are ways to finance the change, as will be shown later. What we first have to decide as a nation is whether we want to plan now for legislation to be financed in the 1990s that will help families.

There is what many regard as a moral question to consider: *should* the federal government help a woman stay home to care for her children or, if she goes out to work, to help her find and pay for adequate child care? Surely it is moral and wise and ultimately prudent economically to help give better care to the nation's children. European nations that share some financial responsibility with parents for the upbringing of children do not report social upheaval or moral decay; quite the contrary. Helping families should definitely be a priority of both federal and state government.

As Sen. Moynihan points out, the $40 billion figure can be viewed as an example of "the extent to which the tax system has shifted against low- and moderate-income families in the postwar years." He also proposes that we could regard an increase in the exemptions as "not so much changing things as restoring what was once in place."[16]

In considering cost, it is also important to think in terms of *social* cost. Decades of child development research strongly indicate that poor care

> has lasting negative effects on the intellectual and socio-emotional development of the children experiencing such care. It has been associated with cognitive and language deficits, as well as difficulties with social relationships.[17]

Some areas of the nation are already seeing community problems directly related to situations in which there is not poor care, but *no care* at all for school-age or "latchkey children."

> It has been estimated that sixty percent of the fires intentionally set in Oakland [California] are set by kids. Of these fires set by kids the vast majority occur during the hours between the close of the school day and the arrival at home of a working parent. These fires range from the accidental fires resulting from children's natural curiosity about fire, to those of the repeat offender who sees fire as a means for him to control some power in an otherwise powerless environment.[18]

One of the most persuasive arguments for increasing dependent tax exemptions is that it would lessen the burden on existing child care facilities. Those women with infants and preschoolers who feel emotional distress at leaving their children in someone else's care would be able to stay home, thus freeing day care space for women who, for whatever reason, feel that they must work. Many experts in the child care field believe that increased competition could go far in improving child care in this country.

With an increase in the dependent tax exemption, women with two or three dependents who continued working would have more money in their pockets each payday and could afford to be more choosy. It is true that low-quality care does not always correspond to low price. There are sitters who charge very little and give wonderful care. But often the better-trained and experienced the care giver and the brighter and more well-equipped the space for care, the more you pay. A slight increase in competition might help to weed out mediocre care givers or inspire them to make some improvements in the care they provide.

The idea of parents' having more expendable dollars for day care also increases the chances that the pay of high-quality day care providers will become commensurate with the physical, emotional, and intellectual demands of the job. They could be given health insurance, sick time, and paid vacations—basic benefits that workers at even some of the best child care centers do not have.

But an increase in pocket money for mothers continuing to work would not be enough to reform child care in the United States. We need significant, widespread changes. Even if half the mothers now working outside the home quit, the nation would still need extensive improvements in the way young children are cared for outside their homes.

Establishing State Regulatory Agencies

In establishing standards for the care of children by someone outside the family, legislators should glean ideas from the excellent recommendations made before the Select Committee hearings. To start, a federal mandate is needed for all states to regulate all day care centers and homes (*day care homes* means baby-sitters in their own homes caring for children—this is also called *family home care* or *family day care*). However, rather than policing the individuals and groups providing care, the agencies should be cooperative and supportive, enhancing the professionalism of providers. They should employ personnel "trained not only in regulations and compliance functions but in giving direct support or referrals in the areas of business management, obtaining affordable liability insurance for homes, buying into health plans, forming credit unions, organizing basic first aid and CPR (cardiopulmonary resuscitation) training, linking with school district supports."[19]

In my ideal conception of child care reform, these agencies would be called Resource, Referral, and Regulation Agencies (RRRA—I know, it sounds like a cheer.) Many of the recommendations made before the Select Committee on Children, Youth, and Families could be included. Agencies could:

Coordinate distribution of surplus foods to day care homes and centers

Organize under the auspices of the federal Department of Education and state boards of education so that early childhood care would be considered part of the public education system, not "welfare"

Encourage care for infants in day care homes

Cooperate with county and city parks administrations, recreation departments, and outdoor preserves to provide recreation for children, especially latchkey children

Encourage the education and training of child care providers in all types of outside care

Establish a referral system for parents; encourage their involvement in day care programs they choose

Encourage the use of volunteers, particularly senior citizens, to "spell" day care providers for four hours a week so that they can have time for pertinent reading and training, as well as rest

Organize latchkey programs in already existing buildings, like public schools, churches, and recreation centers; set up a telephone hotline for those latchkey children who remain at home after school

Publish low-cost pamphlets on subjects like discipline and group play for child care providers through the Government Printing Office

Fine anyone operating a day care center or home who is not registered

Give temporary registrations for six months to those who comply with registration "in the spirit of the law," working with those providers in order to satisfy registration requirements

Avoid establishing physical standards for day care homes and centers that are so restrictive that they discourage the desire to provide care

Keep records of how many child care providers are in the state

Halt federal and state assistance to any local regulation agency that does not comply with federal standards, particularly in health and safety standards

These regulating agencies would obviously have strict standards, but at the same time, they would focus on acting as a cooperative effort of parents, providers, the individual state, and the federal government. They would be resource centers above all else.

In California and several other states, there are already organizations of home day care providers, called Family Day Care Associations, that publish newsletters, update lists of baby sitters, share ideas on how to care for groups of preschoolers, and stay abreast of new state laws, child development night courses and weekend workshops. Such organizations or networks do a great deal to help sitters caring for children in their homes to think of themselves as professionals who provide an important service for their communities.[20]

Day care authority Grace Mitchell has urged that child care licensing be viewed as a resource "rather than as a threat" and personnel as "consultants, advisors, and supporters."[21] Licensing or any other kind of regulation becomes a problem when, for example, laws require that a day care home be accessible to the handicapped when no handicapped children are present or require that every child be poured an eight-ounce glass of milk at lunch when the three-year-olds being cared for can't get down more than four ounces at a sitting. It has been estimated that over 80 percent of family day care in private homes is "underground," and apparently this happens largely because of the restrictiveness of present licensing procedures.[22] Creating state regulatory agencies that are consulting, training, and referral centers would do much to increase knowledge about how children are being cared for outside the home, to give support to the child care profession, and to improve the care itself.

The big question is, how can funds be allocated for state regulatory agencies with the least amount of federal bureaucracy and expense? Many of us who began making our livings during the Great Society era of expanded government spending are very reluctant to encourage the feeding of any more federal bureaucracies. It might be best, then, if the funds for agencies overseeing day care in each state came through Human Services Block Grants (HSBG) in conjunction with the Department of Education. The block grant system is already intact so possibly bureaucratic expenses could be minimized.

Facing an enormous federal deficit, we have become a cost-conscious nation. So, no matter how the administration of a program is handled, the biggest question is "How can we afford to fund any care outside the home?"

In responding to the question U.S. Representatives Bliley, Coats, Wolf, and Vucanovich have answered with another question: "How can we afford not to fund [children's] care?"[23] Consider for a moment what the federal government does fund. Thus far it has subsidized the railroads, the shipping industry, the airlines, exporters of steel, iron, and textiles, dairy and produce farmers, the nuclear power industry, and the defense industry, among others.[24] Critics of the move to increase the dependent tax exemption to help both mothers at home and those who work outside the home have sometimes said that the increase would be "like subsidizing motherhood." We have to decide as a nation what we think is worthwhile "subsidizing."

Using any funds at all to enable states to regulate child care has been critizised as an inappropriate area for federal involvement. Yet as education professor Dr. Bettye Caldwell of the University of Arkansas has pointed out,

It is incomprehensible that federal regulations exist to regulate the meat we eat, the cars we buy, and the airplanes we fly on, but not the quality and safety of the programs that care for our children.[25]

Redefining Our Funding Priorities

We need to find some way to finance an increase in the dependent tax exemption and to finance state Resource, Referral and Regulation Agencies. There have been a number of suggestions to facilitate this, among them raising citizens' local taxes or taxing local businesses $5–$10 a year for every employee with a child in day care. We might also consider reordering the country's priorities and spending patterns. It is another national irony that we spend billions of dollars on national defense, defending, among others, our young, yet in so doing, we now feel financially unable to care for many of them adequately, to defend the right of all children to safety, security, and equal education.

Nearly 50 percent of the people in the United States believes that we are spending too much on defense. But it is not just the inefficiency and excessive spending of the military that is the problem. It is also the role of private defense contractors and various powerful corporations. Rep. Patricia Schroeder has called defense contractors the "welfare queens of the eighties." Corporate welfare is another problem. It includes uncollected corporate tax revenues, unpaid government loans, indirect subsidies, research grants, and rescue packages for banks and important corporations, and has been estimated at costing the nation $80–$100 billion yearly. When defense contracts and other related defense spending are added, the total figure is estimated to be as high as $140 billion.[26] For every dollar collected from private citizens for personal income tax, only 23¢–32¢ is collected in corporate income taxes.[27] Although some economic benefits from these practices may theoretically filter down to us ordinary folk, the facts are nonetheless disturbing.

Some advocates of day care have suggested that parents and others who care about children become educated as to where elected officials stand and vote accordingly. But cleaning up corruption and waste and then recovering defense dollars for a different kind of defense for children is not as easy for elected officials to do as it might sometimes appear. There is also the problem of economic entrenchment: many people depend for their livelihood on the military-industrial complex. Navy yards, universities, army installations, and military training schools all employ private citizens and bolster the economies of individual communities. In the Los Angeles area alone,

125,000 civilian occupations are related to the defense industry. So although some of these occupations might contribute to duplication or inefficiency, they are tough to get rid of. There are some observers of American life and government who fear that as a nation we are incapable of change, that once an agency or industry becomes entrenched it can't ever be removed. Colorado Governor Richared D. Lamm fears America is "a great Gulliver held down by a thousand special-interest Lilliputians."[28]

This is what I guess could be called pessimistic realism, and though intellectually I can identify with it, I hope it is not correct. It has been said that "one hallmark of a civilized society is its willingness to care for its . . . dependent young."[29] In a country as wealthy as ours, there is money that could be redistributed so that we are defending the young in a new sense. I would hope that whichever situation we as individuals embrace—staying home with our children or working outside the home while our children are cared for by others—we will prove ourselves as a society to be civilized.

10

Conclusion:
Moving beyond the Traditional

NO matter how our government responds to the plight of the family today, women who are mothers are responsible for dealing with the conflicts in their lives. In finding the balance between caring for their families at home and providing income for their needs, it might be helpful for modern women to look beyond the conventional definition of *traditional* to what truly *is* traditional: a blending of home and work. To most people, the word *traditional* brings to mind a family with father as sole breadwinner and mother as nurturer, spending her days exclusively caring for children and making the home a place of repose. People using the term this way often seem to think they are talking about a familial configuration that has existed for centuries; that it is "natural" or immutable. Yet this conception of the traditional woman and her family is actually relatively new. In the United States it was common for only a century or so and only among certain classes.

During most of the history of the United States, a mother's primary, traditional function has been *to contribute to the family's economic survival while caring for her children.* She did this in the home in a variety of ways: producing goods for family members so that they would not have to buy outside the home at higher prices; producing additional goods to sell to others; assisting in a spouse's business; running a cottage industry, and sometimes employing hired girls or neighbors to help; or (especially in the first half of the twentieth century), economizing carefully in order to save rather than make money. In some periods, the economic dimension to the mother's role was a brutal one, as in the lives of nineteenth-century New York sweatshop seamstresses who were grossly exploited workers. At other times, the role of women was a congenial blending of tasks that saved or brought in money; the challenge of raising children was an integral part of this role.[1]

Today in staying home to rear their children themselves, women are moving beyond historical tradition to find fulfillment in various areas of their lives. The entrepreneurial businesses and the creative economizing they engage in are not prescribed for them in the way that farming tasks or assistance with a husband's trade were many decades ago. Women do have many choices open to them and have the opportunity to be truly liberated, as hackneyed as that word may now sound.

Women's Historical Roles

At this point it will be useful to review the history of women and work and of women in the home to understand some of the conventions, assumptions, and prejudices that influence American life to this day. It was not until the mid to late nineteenth century that society encouraged women to consider the rearing and educating of children as their primary concern at home—what many people now think of as the traditional mothering role. The change occurred for a variety of complicated political, social, and economic reasons. But one impetus for the change was a growing concern for the problem of "hooliganism" in both cities and rural areas. Young boys without supervision—hooligans—were guilty of vandalism and generally reprobate behavior. Their sisters were sometimes in the streets for reasons other than vandalism.

Social reformers believed that if low- and moderate-income women were able to spend more time attending to these children and teenagers, some social problems could be alleviated. This idea began in England among the middle and upper-middle classes who were gaining in numbers and in political and social influence. The idea spread to the United States and was embraced by the social reformers of the late nineteenth century. So a "tradition" was born, of the mother as educator and authority in the home. At its best, it eroded the notion that women were not much higher than beasts of burden; it gave them status and their own realm: the home. At its worst, it became a genteel prison for intelligent, spirited women. But it became a goal among all classes. The Industrial Revolution and the growth of labor unions, with their emphasis on a "family wage" to be earned by male breadwinners, made it possible for an increasing percentage of the population to achieve this goal by the twentieth century.[2]

There are some misconceptions about what family life was like in the nineteenth and early twentieth centuries. One of the most prevalent is the myth of the "extended family" in the United States. Until the medical advances of the twentieth century increased the life span of the elderly, most young children's grandparents had died by the time they were born or did so shortly afterward. Even in families in which the grandparents were still alive, younger members were mobile, moving fifty miles away from the family homestead—or five hundred. The "extended family" was simply not as common in the United States as it was in southern and eastern Europe. And, at that, plenty of Italian and Polish families left Mama behind in the old country when they emigrated to the New World.

It is also important to remember that in spite of all that has been said about the "bored housewife," the average woman in the late nineteenth century and in the first half of the twentieth century had a great deal to do: tending gardens; canning and preserving fruits, vegetables, and meats; sometimes taking care of chickens and other small animals; making clothing; caring for children; sometimes educating children; and, particularly in the country, working to produce or grow something to sell. If a married woman worked for pay outside the home or took in work (like laundry), it was usually menial, low-paying drudgery that she did because she was poor. Having a wife who worked became almost a stain on a man's character, and the widowed working woman was often an object of pity.

There was little encouragement for women to become professionals, though for a time, it looked as though this might change in the 1920s, especially at some of the women's colleges. In the early twenties, Smith College founded the Institute to Coordinate Women's Interests to help educated women have both a family and career; however, it lasted only six years. Often college-educated women who wanted a professional career were celibate or married late and remained childless.[3]

Though for decades it was common for young working-class women to hold a job prior to marriage and for well-educated middle- and upper-middle-class women, both married and single, to work hard at volunteer jobs, it was not until World War II that married women worked outside the home in significant numbers. By V-J Day, married women outnumbered unmarried women in the work force for the first time in U.S. history. After the war, those women left the work force voluntarily; were forced out; or, tragically for some war widows, were pushed out of high-paying industry jobs into low-paying "women's work." The reasons for this were various: some economic, some "patriotic," some plain sexist. The pay inequities that had been common for decades persisted. The Equal Rights Amendment, which had first been proposed in 1923, looked as if it might pass as a "thank you" to women for their war effort, but it did not.

However, one result of married women's working outside the home during the war was that afterwards, there was a steady increase in the entrance of married, middle-aged, middle-class women into the work force. It was acceptable and respectable for a woman whose job of raising children was essentially over to get a job outside the home. Without any strong feminist movement urging them on, the numbers of middle-aged women entering the work force, mostly in teaching and clerical work, steadily grew in the postwar years.[4]

In the 1960s and 1970s the combination of high inflation and increased Social Security and personal taxes caused many younger families to feel that they needed two paychecks in order to maintain a middle-class standard of living. The growing divorce rate made it necessary for still more women, including those with babies, to join the full-time work force.

It is my belief that these economic and social realities *coincided* with the burgeoning women's movement, but were not necessarily caused by it. The movement offered ideological support for women who were young mothers who also wanted to go back to work. But it is my belief that had the women's movement of the 1960s and 1970s never taken place, there would still have been a large increase in the number of women with children in the work force today. Inflation, no-fault divorce, the low tax exemption for dependents, and the fact that so many of us grew up accustomed to a middle-class life-style have been the significant influences on the decision of many women to leave young children to go out to work. The women's movement gave us the theoretical reasons to work, but the economic and social realities would have been the same.

We responded to the realities the way women have for centuries—by finding a way to bring income into the family. The trouble was and is that in the last hundred and fifty years, the means of earning an income has moved from the home to spheres outside the home in business and industry. In the coming decades, as chapter 8 pointed out, this situation may well change. Let's hope it does, because what the average working mother has experienced in the last ten years has hardly been liberating. There are murmurings, growing louder by the day, that some women may have lost as much—or more—than they've gained.

Misunderstandings between the Generations

One of the things that may have been lost is something that, ironically, the rhetoric of the 1960s women's movement referred to a great deal: sisterhood. I see growing polarities between young women and older women; mothers who "work" and mothers at home who "don't work"; child care providers and the mothers of the children they care for. I first became aware of the polarity between young and old when I was working and found myself being misunderstood by older people. When I told anyone over fifty that I worked, they sometimes gave unsolicited opinions, acting as if I were deliberately doing something awful to my children. If I explained that I didn't want to leave my kids but had to, this provoked a pitying response, which I found irritating. Pointing out that my job was a likeable one caused them to revert to treating me like a selfish destroyer of the home. It was very frustrating. Somehow, to them it was okay to leave your children if you hated your job, but if you liked it, you were suspect.

There are always misunderstandings between the generations, but they seem to have become greater. There is sometimes jealousy on the part of older women because of the material things that some working women have. And some young women seem to think that older and middle-aged women have nothing to teach a new generation of mothers.

It is no wonder that some older women feel resentful, since some young working women with children (and without) act as if older women were once exploited, uncreative, and smothering as housewives and mothers, as if they had been "nonpersons." This attitude can be pretty insulting, particularly to the women of the 1950s who were well-educated and considered themselves resourceful and creative in the home.

I think that to a certain extent mine was a generation of know-it-alls; we weren't keen on the tradition of the younger generation receiving information from the older. If our mothers or grandmothers told us about pain in childbirth we viewed them with tolerant amusement. After all, *we* had Lamaze. We would therefore have "contractions," not "labor pains." We would "stay on top of the contractions," we would breathe fast and never "lose control." Some of us had rude awakenings in our less than perfect Lamaze birthings.

When mothers and grandmothers tried to tell us that having a child would change our whole lives and our marriages, or that we would feel an attachment for our babies like none we'd ever felt before, some of us figured that they "hadn't had much else in their lives." When they warned us that the first few weeks after having a baby we'd be more busy and tired than we'd ever been, we thought *they* were ignorant, not us. After all, times had changed; women had changed. But it never occurred to us that babies hadn't changed or that we might search forever and never find "the perfect person to take care of the baby":

> Babies have not changed their nature in the course of human history. They have not been liberated by the changing family styles of the past decades. . . . It has taken millions of research dollars to find out what anybody's grandmother knew 50 years ago. Babies know their parents and prefer them to other people as early as the first few weeks of life.[5]

For those women who divorced after several years of marriage and a child or two, the concern of our parents about our not insisting on alimony or the family house was met with protests that we would not be "leeches"; we would do fine on our own. In dividing possessions equally in a no-fault divorce, women did not recognize that they would not have an equal chance with their former husbands in the marketplace for pay or positions commensurate with their education or abilities.

We had much to learn from older, experienced women. They could have taught us a lot of what we've learned the hard way if we had only believed that they were *worth* listening to, if we had only been less arrogant.

As part of the early research for this book I interviewed older "career women" to try to understand what it was like to combine paying work and child rearing two generations ago. But I discovered that none of the impressive women I interviewed had gone out to work before their children were in kindergarten. One of the women had strong opinions about the young women in the office she was about to retire from who left their children to work: "They have a baby and come back a few weeks later. They feel confined; they miss people at work and a regular paycheck. And they don't want to go through the adjustment to motherhood that everybody goes through when they're at home with a baby."

These same young mothers may, of course, cry in the parking lot every day the first week they come back. But to older women it looks as if children's lives are being sacrificed for money, and maybe some of them are. One flinty, resourceful widow who had lost her husband in World War II and supported their three small children on a widow's benefits and a variety of at-home jobs was highly critical of mothers leaving their children. "They have to buy clothes instead of making them. I used to make summer dresses out of flour sacks. . . . They have to have disposable diapers instead of washing out cloth diapers. They're used to things being so easy. And you have to have a paycheck to buy what's easy."

A woman in her seventies from New Jersey who had worked for almost forty years, but only after her last child entered public school, made similar comments: "I think young people in this country have lost the art of waiting. They want so much, so soon, and they truly believe this is the way it's got to be: a nice apartment, new furniture, a full china closet, then a beautiful house—all before they're twenty-eight. I was forty before we owned our own home."

It is no wonder that as a nation we cannot get together to solve the problems of those children whose mothers work. There is valid criticism of the younger generation by the older generation, but there is also jealousy and lack of understanding. Older women need to recognize that the reason a working mother may be wearing a fashionable suit is that she has to dress like that for work. Or that she may have some extra cash because although for financial reasons she needed only a part-time job, she was unable to get anything but a full-time position.

At the same time, women suffering separation pangs from their babies shouldn't have to pretend that they are not. Those suffering stress or uncertainty should admit it to older relatives and neighbors. If nothing else, they would at least no longer come across as cold, heartless princesses of narcissism. They might also get some concrete help in the form of backup babysitting.

Those of us who got out of the rat race and are at home need to pay more attention to how women over fifty managed things like raising three children on a postal worker's salary. I don't think that the higher dependent tax exemption is the only way to help at-home mothers. Admittedly, the days are over when a young woman learned from older women all the tasks and traditions that she needed to conduct her life. But we could still gain from each other. The polarity that now exists does nothing for anyone.

Women Who "Work" and Women Who "Don't"

Another division is between women of the same generation: mothers who work full-time outside the home and those who don't. Asking a woman I've just met at a cocktail party how she spends her day is something I may never try again. Women who "don't work"—that is, work at home as mothers—sometimes visibly bridle. Mothers who work full-time outside the home often feel compelled to mention how worthwhile their work is or how wonderful their day care center is. The feelings about both life-styles have heated up tremendously in the last several years:

Nice mothers shouldn't fight. So the dissension between working and non-working mothers is often disguised by a pretense of tolerance for the other point of view. . . . But, like religion, absolute conviction precludes any real acceptance of the other belief. If one side is right, the other must be wrong.[6]

Each has ideas about how the world may view them negatively:

> Working women are stung and enraged by the guilt-provoking suggestion that their careers are more important to them than their children; that if they loved their babies more they'd be willing to put their work aside. And fulltime mothers are angered and shaken by the low esteem with which many career women regard them.[7]

Women in each camp (it's hard to get away from the embattled images) find that what they do is unacceptable to *someone.*

Within the ranks of full-time working mothers, an additional division exists between women who have "ordinary" clerical or teaching jobs and professional women who have "high-powered" jobs. The latter are almost always in business, banking, or industry, so those in fields traditionally dominated by women are not regarded as "high powered" or "on top." What this means is that an elite has formed among working women. Generally, the more time a woman spends with men in a male-dominated occupation, the higher the status. Women who work with other women or with children are considered lower in status. Consequently, teaching school, one of the most stimulating and demanding jobs around—and one that allows you to do some of the work at home and have the summer free for your own children—is looked down upon by bright young women.

Marian Blum points out an interesting irony resulting from this situation that can be seen in day care centers:

> Many contemporary parents, some of whom consider themselves feminists, emphasize the importance of nonstereotyped role models. And then, they enroll their children in institutions where, all too frequently, depressed women do what is perceived as menial work. The role model of the successful woman in the gray flannel suit with the leather briefcase does not work at the day-care center.[8]

A day care worker or a baby-sitter can feel uncomfortable with the accomplishments of a professional woman. On the other hand, a mother, especially a new mother, can feel inexperienced compared with a woman who has over the years cared for dozens of children. In the words of a former day care worker, there can be "a clash in social class" and therefore sometimes "a clash in values." She thinks that there needs to be "a good fit," but with so much of day care underground and underpaid, this goal can be tough to accomplish. Consequently, hostility sometimes exists between the two people concerned with the well-being of the child. The mother needs understanding, and the child care provider needs respect.

Class Divisions—Pushing Poor Women out of the Home

In the day care issue another problem encourages polarity and social division. When advocates of federally subsidized child care discuss the programs, they often sound as if they want to do everything they can to push poor and lower-middle income women out of the home. For example, some day care proposals have included incentives to poor parents, who choose the least expensive care for their children, which, of course, often means the worst care. Many child care experts are warning of the danger of the United States' becoming a nation that supports a two-tier system of child care in which the working poor have the worst for their children and upper-middle-income working couples have the best.[9] This situation could have unfortunate social consequences in the future, apart from any objection that it is unfair to the children.

But in the hundreds of pages of testimony on child care before the House Select Committee on Children, Youth, and Families there was little discussion of the benefits of keeping a low-income mother at home with her small children. Apart from the efforts of Congresswomen Schroeder and Mikulski, inadequate efforts have been made to encourage flexible working conditions that would allow a poor woman to spend as much time as possible at home with her children.

When I was teaching in Boston in the 1970s, I met three mothers—two married and one single—who were at home with their children in spite of the fact that the families were poor. They lived in housing projects on small incomes, and one was helped along with food stamps and AFDC (Aid to Families with Dependent Children). They were at home because, as one woman put it, "I'm the only thing between my kid and the drug pusher on the street. As long as I'm *here*, my kids have got a chance."

Many of us often equate "poor woman at home" with welfare and resist the idea of increasing the welfare rolls. But we need to consider that perhaps encouraging low-income women into the work force is not necessaily the best thing to do for the health of individual families or the nation. Poor women might benefit more than any group from at-home paying work. Therefore, it seems wise to expend more energy helping these women to become self-supporting at home, or outside the home during hours when their children are in school. This approach could ultimately result in saving money in both subsidized day care and on the welfare rolls. It could also help to prevent a situation in which only middle- and upper-income women can stay home with their children.

Stereotyping of Women at Home

Sometimes the polarities and social divisions are more funny than sad. Since deciding to stay home, I have found that all kinds of assumptions are sometimes made about the woman at home: that she is conservative in her politics, religion, and social views; that she's probably rich; and that maybe her husband doesn't "let" her work outside the home. For example, I once appeared on a television program about the crisis in child care in the United States and was presented by the program's host as a mother who solved her day care problems by working at home. At no time did I express any political or social opinions that were either left or right during the early part of the discussion. Yet halfway through the program I was referred to as "representing the Right" and then asked a question. I tried to keep from choking and finally, unable to think of any rejoinder, simply shrugged and looked blank. But I have since found that it is not unusual for people to ask an at-home mother if she is "you know, a Phyllis Schlafley sort of person?" If you stay home with your children, some people will automatically place you in a right-wing slot.

In fact, there are women at home who are NOW officers, neoliberals, neoconservatives, moderates, trade unionists, anarchists. They are left-wing, right-wing, "pro-life," "pro-choice," anti-ERA, pro-ERA. As *Welcome Home* editor, Cheri Loveless has said, "The choice to stay at home crosses all political and socioeconomic boundaries. You cannot pigeonhole us as a group."[10] In the future, women need to recognize that their progress in gaining equality and respect as a sex will be impeded if the majority of them have attitudes and actions that increase rather than minimize their differences.

Fantasy versus Reality

Not only are women held back by misunderstandings among themselves, but also by the persistence of an old and self-defeating fantasy. A couple of years after I quit work, I read a book entitled *The Cinderella Complex*. When I first heard about it, I felt a little uneasy and considered whether wanting to be take care of, without realizing it, was one of my motivations for staying home. But after reading the book I decided that I had quit not so that someone else would take care of me, but so that I could take care of others.

Still, the message behind *The Cinderella Complex*—that women cannot expect to be swept away by a Prince Charming and must prepare themselves to be self-supporting—is compelling and instructive for all of us. One of the major goals of the women's movement should continue to be encouraging teenaged and young women to attain the highest education possible in order to be self-supporting. Unfortunately, there are indications that so far, that message has not gotten through to everyone.

At a conference of the Girls Clubs of America in the spring of 1985, delegates reported on the continuing influence of the Cinderella fantasy on young girls: "These young women cling to the notion that they need not prepare for a career because they will be provided for—royally."[11] According to Margaret Gates, executive director of Girls Clubs, "They expect new opportunities for women in the workplace to provide good jobs, [but] at the same time they stay away from math, science, and computer courses because they're for boys, not girls." Delegates pointed out that the problem is exacerbated by the practice of individual communities and public schools to "convey a subtle message that girls are less able than boys."[12]

Obviously, we need to do a lot of education—in both subject matter and reality—or our younger sisters will make little progress. In interviewing divorced women in their early thirties, I was struck by how many of them had grown up in upper-middle-income families and yet as single parents were in a low-income group. Unless we make some changes, the so-called feminization of poverty will continue to plague us and may widen in scope.

At the same time, we have to guard against a tendency in the women's movement to regard a career as a means to great joy and fulfillment. We have to make it clear that for the ordinary working mother the reality is just to try to make a buck at work and to keep everybody's socks matched at home. There is really not much glamour in most jobs, and when there is, a good deal of stress is usually involved too. This doesn't mean that life is grim; it just means that life isn't simple and a job, like everything else, is usually both good and bad. If we are willing to look, there are often a series of answers that emerge from the conflicts, responsibilities, and joys of the different seasons of a woman's life. We need to avoid rigid responses. According to writer and psychologist Elaine Heffner:

> Women were for a time told that the only way to be a real woman was through motherhood. In order to be whole they would have to sacrifice those parts of themselves that longed for expression in other ways. Now women are being told that in order to be whole they must sacrifice the impulse to mother. . . . Neither view addresses the full range of women's feelings. . . . We

appear to believe that perfection is an attainable state. When we encounter a problem that grows out of the conflicts of living, we imagine the problem is the result of the existing solution, rather than part of life itself. We are quick to conclude that an opposite solution would achieve the life free of pain that we are seeking.[13]

The solution to "'liberate' women from the mother role rather than by helping them become successful within it"[14] is an example of this kind of thinking.

We need to stop listening to those feminists who tell us how it's "supposed to be" for all working women. Listening to them and following their lead has been a little like taking flying lessons from people who don't have pilots' licenses. Many of the most famous feminists of the '60s who said we could have it all were childless and unmarried. The few who had families either had the money to hire housekeepers and other help while they worked outside the home or they stayed home most of the time that their children were small and merely imagined what it would have been like to have an interesting full-time job. In short, many feminist leaders were more ignorant than arrogant. They simply did not have the *experience* to instruct us. It is no wonder that today many working mothers feel as if they are flying off course.

Those who feel caught in the working-mom rat race need to know that combining full-time work with motherhood *is* hard. We need to admit this to other women, to husbands and lovers, to bosses, to parents, to our mothers-in-law—to everyone who has anything to do with our lives. By acknowledging this, I do not mean whining or beating our breasts, but stating clearly that having it all all at once is exhausting for the average woman. If we do this, some changes may become possible: a half-day or job-sharing arrangement at our present job; computer-based projects at home; backup baby-sitting from an elderly neighbor; greater responsibility from a spouse for home and children; and perhaps the enlightenment of some younger women.

But finally to make the communication leap to admitting to others as well as to ourselves that Supermom doesn't live in *this* house requires one important thing: power. We all hear so much rhetoric about power that the word has "become heavy with the weight of emotional and political overtones."[15] But in the best sense of the word, if a woman is powerful, she is confident about her life choices and strong enough to get what she needs. It takes power to admit that a problem exists and to work out a solution. An unhappy working wife and mother who says, "I'd like to quit but I just can't" is often behaving in a passive, powerless way. She can make an effort to look at options and find alternatives. If she fails in the effort, then she has to work at accepting the situation and move on, but at least in making the effort, she is behaving like a strong, free woman.

Gains from the Women's Movement

In sometimes criticizing the women's movement, particularly the radical element, I do not mean to deny what we have gained as a direct result of it. As individuals, women can now get credit ratings and bank loans on their own. We have a better chance for admittance to law school or medical school. There are legal mechanisms now in place to discourage sexual harassment on the job. We enjoy marriages to men who are often more involved in the birth and rearing of children than their fathers were.

As a society, we have gained because the country is now less likely to lose out on using the talent and intelligence of half our population in areas outside the home. A young woman with high intelligence and great dexterity is more likely to become a surgeon today, for example. But we have not gone far enough to enable her to conduct a half-day practice once she's performed brilliantly in the operating room at 8:00 A.M. We have not, as a society, recognized that if a young man who is an M.D. serves in the Navy for six years after completing his internship, he is praised; while a young woman who is an M.D. and serves as a full-time mother for six years after completing her internship is criticized. We do not regard her as serving her country. We do not think of her time at home as a period when she may be learning new skills that can help her in her job when she returns.

Career Women and Pressure

We put tremendous pressure on those women who make it to the top in professions to keep their noses to the grindstone. Some men who go though three years of law school later become stockbrokers, real estate investors, or travel agents. The fact that a man has a background in law but goes into something other than the law is typically regarded as "interesting." A woman who does the same thing, or simply takes off for a few years to have children and then returns to the profession, is not quite playing fair. After all, she "took up space" in law school and then didn't use her degree.

Ironically, some of the top professions lend themselves best to half-days and "mother's hours" because of a heavy reliance on scheduling by appointment. Nevertheless, the pressure is often greatest in these professions to keep strictly conventional office hours. Our society would benefit greatly if we could reexamine the various conventions and assumptions that govern working customs.

Some people have called for business and the professions to become more sensitive to women's needs and more responsive to the American family. However, some of the specific proposals to make this possible are naive. A business is a business is a business. Its purpose is to make money in the most efficient way possible. Large, wealthy corporations will establish on-site day care facilities when they see that it improves production. Both big and small business employers will establish flex-time and job-sharing when they see that it is to their benefit to do so, and when we *tell* them how badly this is needed. We have the chance now to change slowly what has been unfair to us, but we will not succeed by demanding what is unrealistic or naive or unfair to the business community.

In some situations women of talent and ambition will have to strike out on their own. The message for these women in the latter part of this century will be: If you can't beat 'em, forget 'em. It is therefore important that we safeguard and promote our right to earn money in our own homes; to revive and make strong the American tradition of independence and entrepreneurship.

American society does face many changes, but not necessarily of the kind some demographers and feminist spokeswomen are predicting. It is estimated that by the year 1990, 75 percent of preschool children in the United States will have a mother in the labor force. But it's also predicted that half the jobs in the United States will be part-time by 1990.[16]

A number of factors could militate against increasing numbers of young women joining the labor force full-time. For one thing, millions of women are getting fed up with full-time work outside the home, and by the end of the 1980s they may be very fed up. I think they will seek alternatives to full-time work outside the home. A second important factor is the technological change that may make more telecommunication jobs at home possible, even likely. Futurist Alvin Toffler believes that social changes will occur today and in the future to encourage an increase in electronic cottage industry growth: the transportation crisis in North American cities and their attendant air pollution and parking problems; the escalating costs of real estate and office maintenance; the interest in small city and rural life; the average worker's distaste for commuting; and, in the midst of a high divorce rate, the desire to "glue the family unit together again," with both children and parents helping each other at home.[17] As work at home using a computer becomes more common, I think it is possible that women who cannot do this specific type of work will search for some other way to combine paying work with child rearing at home.

One additional factor may bring more working mothers home to stay with their children, and that is the tide of social opinion that seems to be turning away from radical feminism, from what writer Linda Gray Sexton has dubbed the "feminist mystique"[18] and one of the women I interviewed called the "feminist mystaque." Many women of my generation have finally realized that they cannot bear a child or go through the anxious years of the adoption process, and then leave these children with ease—either physical or emotional—to work outside the home. It isn't just that children are a responsibility; they are—more than anything—heart pullers. We've found, as our grandmothers could have told us, that it's hard racing ahead on the fast track—or, for that matter, on the slow track—when a baby is pulling our hearts the other way.

Appendix A: Resources

Books

Chapter 1

Where's My Happy Ending?, Lee Morical. Reading, Mass.: Addison-Wesley, 1984.

Chapter 2

Career and Conflict, A Woman's Guide to Making Life Choices, Anne Russell and Patricia Fitzgibbons. Englewood Cliffs, N.J.: Prentice-Hall, 1982.

Chapter 3

Choosing Child Care: A Guide for Parents, Stevanne Auerbach. New York: Dutton, 1981. Short, helpful guide for parents who must work.

The Day-Care Dilemma, Marian Blum. Lexington, Mass.: Lexington Books, 1983. Tells you what you need to know but may not want to hear.

Mother Care/Other Care, Sandra Scarr. New York: Basic Books, 1984.

The Parents with Careers Workbook, Rebecca Sager Ashery and Michele Margolin Basen. Washington, D.C.: Acropolis, 1983. Very thorough, with information on how to screen potential child care providers and what to look for in good day care.

Chapter 4

Money Book, Sylvia Porter. New York: Avon, 1976.

The Heart Has Its Own Reasons, Mary Ann Cahill. Franklin Park, Ill.: La Leche League International, 1983.

Mort's Guide to Low Cost Vacations and Lodgings on College Campuses, Mort and Jane Barish, CMG Publishing Co., P.O. Box 630, Princeton, NJ 08540.

Chapter 5

Catalog Sources for Creative People, Margaret A. Boyd. Tucson, Ariz.: H.P. Books, 1981.

Guide to Off Price Shopping, Sue Goldstein. New York: Warner Books, 1984.

Recyclopedia, Robin Simons. Brookings, Oreg.: Sandpiper, 1976.

SOS: Save on Shopping Directory, 10th ed. Iris Ellis. New York: Villard Books, 1985.

You can write for these publications:

Freebie Magazine: The Magazine with Something for Nothing, P.O. Box 20283, Santa Barbara, CA 93120. Great for getting things for kids.

From Deadlines to Diapers: A Career Guide for Successful Homemaking, Tamera Smith Allred. Liberty Press, 500 West/1200 South, Orem, UT 84058.

Globe Pequot Press, Old Chester Rd., Chester, CT 06412. They have a free catalog listing budget-minded books on a variety of subjects.

Chapter 6

Father Feelings, Eliot A. Daley. New York: William Murrow & Co., 1978.

How to Start a Baby Sitting Co-op, Sylvia B. Evans. 906 Hampstead, Richmond, VA 23206. About $2.00.

Mothering, Elaine Heffner. Garden City, N.Y.: Doubleday, 1978.

The Playgroup Handbook, Laura Broad and Nancy Butterworth. New York: St. Martin's Press, 1974.

Welcome Home newsletter, P.O. Box 2208, Merrifield, VA 22116. Well worth the $12.00 a year subscription price.

What is a Wife Worth? Michael H. Minton, with Jean Libman Block. New York: William Murrow, 1983.

Woman at Home, Arlene Rossen Cardozo. Garden City, N.Y.:

Doubleday, 1976. Out of print, but available from public libraries and used book stores. An excellent book.

Chapter 7

Career Changing: The Worry-Free Guide, Linda Kline and Lloyd L. Feinstein. Boston: Little, Brown, 1982. Emphasis is on permanent, full-time jobs, but book could be used by anyone. Good examples of résumés.

The Complete Guide to Job Sharing, Patricia Lee. New York: Walker & Co., 1983.

Part-time Jobs, Viviénne Sernaqué, with Nachman Urieli. New York: Ballantine Books, 1982. Excellent reference. Includes appendixes listing hundreds of jobs in specific categories.

Working Free: Practical Alternatives to the 9 to 5 Job, John Applegath. New York: American Management Association, 1982. Very good, upbeat book.

The Workweek Revolution, Dougles L. Fleuter. Reading, Mass.: Addison-Wesley, 1975. An excellent book for employers to read who need information about flex-time and job sharing and how these programs benefit them.

Chapter 8

"Don't Just Advertise, Publicize." Fact sheet from MHBN, P.O. Box 423, East Meadow, NY 11703.

Earn Money at Home: Over 100 Ideas for Business Requiring Little or No Capital, Peter Davidson. New York: McGraw-Hill, 1982.

Entrepreneurial Mothers, Phyllis Gillis. New York: Rawson Associates, 1983.

Guide to Business Planning, David Bangs and William Osgood. Upstart Publishing Co., Dover, NH 03820; phone 603-749-5071.

The Unabashed Self-Promoter's Guide, Jeffry Lant. Jeffry Lant Associates, 50 Follen St., Suite 507, Cambridge, MA 02138. $31.50 with shipping.

Women Working Home, 2nd ed., Marion Behr and Wendy Lazar. P.O. Box 237CC, Norwood, NJ 07648. Also available through bookstores.

Working from Home, Paul and Sarah Edwards. Los Angeles, Calif.: Jeremy P. Tarcher, distributed by Houghton Mifflin, Boston, 1985.

Worksteads: Living and Working in the Same Place, Jeremy Joan Hewes. New York: Doubleday/Dolphin, 1981. Good for both men and women.

Organizations

Chapter 5

The Cooperative League of the USA (CLUSA), Suite 1100, 1828 L Street NW, Washington, D.C. 20036.

Chicago Area Food Co-op Information Center, P.O. Box 2559, Chicago, IL 60690; phone 312-227-5897.

Acorn Structures (house plans and kits), P.O. Box 250, Concord, MA 01742. Costs $10 for a catalogue.

Home Planners, Inc., 23761 Research Drive, Farmington Hills, MI 48024; and 772 King St. W., Kitchener, Ontario N2G 1E8, Canada. Costs $3 for a catalogue.

Shelter Institute, 38 Center St., Bath, ME 04530; phone 207-442-7938. Two, three, and fifteen week courses, $400–690 a course. Many offered in the summer. Highly recommended.

Chapter 7

Association of Part-Time Professionals, P.O. Box 3419, Alexandria, VA 22303; phone 703-734-7975.

AAUW (American Association of University Women), 2401 Virginia NW, Washington, D.C. 20037; phone 202-785-7700.

Catalyst, 14 E. 60th St., New York, NY 10022; phone 212-759-9700. For information on networks and job counseling.

National Chamber of Commerce for Women, P.O. Box 1132, New York, NY 10159.

YWCA. See local phone book for address and phone number. Workshops on reentering work force and alternative employment opportunities.

For minority women: free or low-cost consulting help on entering the labor force is available at some universities and city or state nonprofit organizations. Call local small business administration or city hall.

Flex-time and job-sharing information by region:

New England—Work Options Unlimited, 645 Boylston St., Boston, MA 02116; phone 617-247-3600.

West Coast—New Ways to Work, 149 Ninth St., San Francisco, CA 94103; phone 415-552-1000.

N.Y./N.J. area—Workshare, Inc., 311 E. 50th St., New York, NY 10022; phone 212-832-7061.

South—Austin Women's Center, 1505 W. 6th, Austin, TX 78703; phone 512-472-3775.

Midwest—Nothing available at this time. Check local phone book.

Nationwide—National Network for Work Time Options, c/o New Ways to Work, 149 9th St., San Francisco, CA 94103.

Chapter 8

Networks:

MHBN (The Mothers' Home Business Network), P.O. Box 423, East Meadow, NY 11554.

NAHB (National Alliance of Homebased Business Women), P.O. Box 306, Midland Park, NJ 07432.

Crafts:

Constance Hallinan Lagan, 35 Claremont Ave., North Babylon, NY 11703; phone 516-661-5181. Inexpensive Marketing Options Reports available on writing for crafts magazines, teaching crafts, and marketing.

Trade Marts:

The Mart, 125th Street, New York, NY, and Trade Mart, Dallas, Texas.

Direct Sales:

Direct Selling Association, 1776 K St. NW, Suite 600, Washington, D.C. 20006.

Entrepreneurial Businesses:

Entrepreneurship Institute, 90 E. Wilson Bridge Rd., Suite 247, Worthington, OH 43805.

SBA (Small Business Administration), central office, 1441 L St. NW, Washington, D.C. 20416; write for free pamphlets on entrepreneurial businesses. See also local SBA, particularly Small Business Development Centers (SBDC). For financing ask about SBA development and expansion grants and how to contact the local Venture Capital Network.

Professional Assistance: SCORE (Service Corps of Retired Executives) and ACE (Active Corps of Executives); free consulting. See SBA for local branch.

Small Business Institutes: Free advice from M.B.A. students at universities and colleges. Ask about these at local SBA office.

AWED (American Women's Economic Development Corporation), $5–$25 for professional consultation by phone, 10:00 A.M. to 5:00 P.M. (EST); phone 800-222-AWED. In Hawaii, Alaska, and New York City, phone 212-692-9100.

NAWBO (National Association of Women Business Owners), for advice on networking and conferences, 645 N. Michigan Ave., Chicago, IL 60611.

For a $5.00 "entrepreneurial kit": Coopers and Lybrand, 2900 One American Square, P.O. Box 82002, Indianapolis, IN 46282.

For a tax kit: Internal Revenue Service (local branch), "Your Business Tax Kit"; free.

Appendix B:
Alternatives to 9–5 Jobs

T HE businesses described below demonstrate how to use skills, resources, and personal interests to earn income. The following five women have fictitious names but real businesses.

A Home Baking Business

Susan Anders had a two-year-old daughter she loved taking care of, a high school diploma, a gift for making great cheesecake, and an extra stove on the back porch of her apartment. When she started André's Gourmet Cheesecakes, she lived in a resort community that had to import cheesecake from bakeries in New York or Boston. She took advantage of the fact that a relative worked in the dairy department of her local supermarket and could get eggs, sour cream, butter, and cream cheese at a discount. Susan bought several springform pans, and after making the rounds of the resort's most expensive restaurants with generous samples of her cheesecake, she was in business.

Five mornings a week, after playing with her daughter for an hour, Susan is ready to mix up and bake her cheesecake. In the afternoon when they're cool, she places them on cardboard rounds, wraps them, and seals them with her gold "André's Cheesecakes" sticker. Her carpenter husband brings home their truck in the middle of the afternoon and looks after their daughter for an hour while Susan delivers her cakes.

Susan does not have a six-figure income. But she does take advantage of the fact that the local restaurants' clientele will pay top dollar for freshly made cheesecake and charges accordingly. She makes enough to supplement her husband's income and occasionally take her husband and daughter out for their own dessert treat.

Computer Consulting and Writing at Home

Marjory Zell makes a much higher income as a computer consultant and writer. She has an eight-year-old and a five-year-old and works from an office that was once a formal dining room. She has a bachelor's degree and had a variety of part-time jobs in and out of the home before she got interested in computers. She took a couple of good computer courses, "played" with a computer that a storekeeper friend had, and got to know some people in her area who made their living working with computers before she bought a small desk computer. She gave free "helping sessions" at the public library on Saturday mornings for adults and children who had just bought new computers and then managed to sell a local newspaper on the idea of a weekly column on computers in exchange for free advertising. She soon became known as an expert.

She now writes instructional manuals on computer software for a large publishing company, teaches courses on how to use computers, and serves as a consultant to area businesses and schools. Marjory uses networking a great deal to get business and to pass on business. She also networks to get free use of the best computer software, telling manufacturers that if she can have free use of their software in her classes, she will, in effect, be encouraging students to buy the manufacturer's products. They get free advertising and promotion, and she gets the software.

Marjory works each morning until her son arrives home from kindergarten, then she takes a long break, and then works another hour or two while he reads or watches "Sesame Street." She does errands and some household chores during a break in the afternoon when her daughter arrives home. She later works another two or three hours in the evening while her husband cares for the children. Marjory makes a very good living, though she points out that she usually works six hours a day and, before publishing deadlines, eight or more a day—something not everyone is willing to do. "But I can do my work in jeans or my bathrobe if I feel like it. I have the freedom to work a lot or a little."

Paralegal Work Partly at Home

Claire Donovan wanted to get out of the house and out of her jeans when she started her own business as a paralegal. She had worked for several years as a legal secretary before giving birth to a son and a daughter. She enjoyed the years at home when her children were babies but felt restless and a little confined as they grew older. She worked part-time as a legal secretary but found that she felt guilty when there was an emergency and she needed time off for her kids. "Feeling guilty and having divided loyalties between my kids and my boss was my main motivation for starting my own business."

Today the main focus of that business is on residential and commercial title searches for attorneys practicing law in the area where Claire and her family live. The work is very precise, and Claire found she could not do it at home because of all the interruptions. She therefore works occasionally at her clients' office and, more often, at a desk at the county office. Since the office is a public building, there is no charge for this space and documents and records she must consult are within easy reach.

At home, Claire has an answering machine to receive calls when she is away and a desk where she can do billing and other record keeping in the afternoon. Though the work is demanding and Claire had to take some difficult courses to qualify as a certified paralegal in her state, she loves the work itself and the stimulation of the people she works with. Currently, the only drawback is that the demand for Claire's services has become so great that she could "easily spend sixty hours a week on the business." Now that her children are both in school, she works about forty hours a week, tailoring her schedule to her children's school hours and extracurricular activities. When too much business comes her way, she refers potential clients to other certified paralegals and, after seven and a half years in the business, she has hired an assistant and given herself the entire month of August for time at home for rest and family.

Buying and Refurbishing Old Houses

Like Claire Donovan, Ann Minotti works outside the home, but her eight-year-old son is often at her side. Five years ago, when she was just divorced, she had a degree in biology, half the money from the sale of her home, and a great reluctance to leave her then two and a half year old to go out to work. She and a friend who was also going through a divorce decided to form a partnership to do something they had talked and dreamed of for years: buying and refurbishing old Victorian houses and renting out the finished rooms to university students and the elderly. Ann had some carpentry skills and had previously taken a couple of courses on the history and restoration of old houses, but most of all, she had a strong commitment to doing interesting work that could include her son.

In order to organize a work crew, Ann and her friend advertised in the local newspaper for women with or without repair and decorating skills and said they could bring their children. The phone "rang off the hook," and Ann was in business. She now buys and refurbishes three-story Victorian houses—about two a year—and does some restoration projects for individual clients as well as some consulting.

People outside the business are still amazed at her success. "The most common question I get about our mom-and-kids crews is 'How can you possibly work with little kids around?' Yet in all the years I've been doing this, we've never had one problem. Kids understand that they can help Mom out by being good, and there's surprisingly little fighting among the children. We keep all dangerous tools away from the kids, instruct them in safety, and let them do some of the work themselves, like spackling nail holes. If one of us has to leave to pick up an older child at school and take him to gymnastics or something, that person just leaves for half an hour and resumes work later."

Ann now has an office with two full-time employees in the town where she has many of her rental properties. When her son was a preschooler, Ann worked with him nearby. Now that he is in school, most afternoons he gets off the school bus at her office instead of at home. She has a snack of home-made cookies and milk for him, which he eats at an office table. He then does his homework while Ann works or, if he has an after-school activity, she drives him to the extracurricular activity and then returns to the office or goes to one of the houses she is refurbishing. Some of the original crew members still work on projects with her, and others have struck out on their own to do the same kind of work. But there are still lots of children at the job sites.

Part-Time Work as a Physical Therapist

As the head of the physical therapy department at a large city hospital, Janet Roberts did not have the kind of profession that would allow her to bring her newborn child to work with her. When she took a maternity leave, she fully intended to simply stay home for a few weeks and then return to work full-time. She was upset to find that she hated leaving her baby all day and was physically exhausted both at work and at home. She had a "hellish" three months before she set up a job-sharing arrangement with another professional in her department who was qualified to divide the management and supervisory responsibilities of the job. "But even this didn't work," she recalls, "because even though I was paid for twenty-five hours a week, I was constantly on the phone on my off-days discussing decisions that had to be made with my job sharer. I was overly conscientious and could not seem to get over the fact that I had once been sole head of this department and had worked sixty hours a week at the job."

After several months, Janet finally decided to make a complete break and go to another hospital as a part-time employee working twenty hours a week with no supervisory responsibilities. "For me this is perfect. I give my all for three days a week and then I'm home, really home. Yet I'm not climbing the walls the way I know I would if I weren't working at all. A lot of people might say I've taken a step down, but I don't give a damn what people say I 'should' be doing. I'm still involved in a profession I love, I'm still contributing to the household economically, and, best of all, I'm spending most of my days with my son, which for me is a step up."

Notes

PREFACE

1. Excerpts from Arlene Rossen Cardozo, *Woman at Home* (Garden City, N.Y.: Double-day, 1976), pp. 3–4. Copyright © 1970 by Arlene Rossen Cardozo. Reprinted by permission of Doubleday & Company, Inc.

1. INTRODUCTION: IS THIS LIBERATION?

1. Lee Morical, *Where's My Happy Ending?* (Reading, Mass.: Addison-Wesley, 1984), p. 49.
2. Betty Friedan, lecture at the University of New Hampshire, March 1982.
3. Lynda Hurst in an article for *Breakthrough* newsletter cited in Betty Friedan, *The Second Stage* (New York: Summit Books, 1981), p. 33.
4. Jane Pauley, quoted in Mary Ann Bucknum Brinley, "The Frustrations of a Working Mother," *McCalls*, November 1984, p. 68.
5. Dan Sperling, "Coming Clean about Our Housework," *USA Today*, October 4, 1984, sec. D, p. 5.
6. Morical, *Where's My Happy Ending?*, p. 29.
7. Lee Bergman, telephone interview, March 9, 1982.
8. Ellen Goodman, "Just Woman's Work?" in *At Large* (New York: Summit Books, 1981), p. 185.
9. Cheri Loveless, telephone interview, June 27, 1984.
10. D. Stanley Eitzen, *Social Problems*, ? :d ed. (Boston: Allyn & Bacon, 1986), in press.
11. Ibid.
12. Rep. Frank Wolf, cited in Carol Felsenthal, "Congress Getting Involved in Day Care Issues," *Chicago Sun Times*, May 6, 1984, p. 18.
13. Dan Rather, "CBS Evening News," April 4, 1984.
14. U.S. Department of Labor, Bureau of Labor Statistics and Women's Bureau (Washington, D.C., March 1985).
15. Cheri Loveless, telephone interview, January 21, 1985.
16. Deborah Churchman, "Women in Business: The New Entrepreneurs," *Christian Science Monitor*, August 26, 1982, p. 15, and Phyllis Gillis, *Entrepreneurial Mothers* (New York: Rawson Associates, 1983), p. 5.

2. THE WORKING-MOM RAT RACE

1. Rachel Tomkins, Testimony before Select Committee on Children, Youth, and Families, Washington, D.C. April 4, 1984 hearing, p. 33.

2. Dr. Estelle Ramey, lecture at Phillips Exeter Academy, Exeter, N.H., June 23, 1983.

3. Lee Morical, *Where's My Happy Endling?* (Reading, Mass.: Addison-Wesley, 1984), p. 128.

4. Dr. Avodah K. Offit, cited in Natalie Gittelson, "Success and Love: Do I Have to Choose?" *McCalls*, November 1982, p. 182.

5. Richard Moore and Elizabeth Marsis, "Sisterhood under Siege," *The Progressive*, January 1985, pp. 30–31. Reprinted by permission from *The Progressive*, 409 East Main Street, Madison, Wisconsin 53703. Copyright © 1984, The Progressive Inc.

6. Patricia L. Dombrink, "The Gender of Success," *Christian Science Monitor*, August 9, 1982, p. 23. Reprinted with permission of the author.

7. Reprinted by permission of the publisher, from Marian Blum, *The Day-Care Dilemma* (Lexington, Mass.: Lexington Books, D.C. Heath and Company, Copyright 1983, D.C. Heath and Company), p. 115.

8. Marjorie Hansen Schaevitz, *The Superwoman Syndrome* (New York: Warner Books, 1984), p. 55.

9. Gay Norton, "When Spouses Pass in the Night," *Family Weekly*, August 7, 1983.

10. Dan Sperling, "Coming Clean about Our Housework," *USA Today*, October 4, 1984, sec. D., p. 5.

11. Anita Shreve, "The Lure of Motherhood," *New York Times Magazine*, November 21, 1982, p. 43.

3. ANXIETY ATTACKS AT THE BABY-SITTER'S DOOR

1. William O'Neil, cited in Carol Hymowitz and Michaele Weissman, *A History of Women in America* (New York: Bantam, 1978), p. 321.

2. See Wayne Eastep, "Nomads of the Desert," *Smithsonian*, December 1984, pp. 46–56, and Bruno Bettelheim, *The Children of the Dream* (New York: Macmillan, 1969).

3. Reprinted by permission of the publisher, from Marian Blum, *The Day-Care Dilemma* (Lexington, Mass.: Lexington, Books, D.C. Heath and Company, Copyright 1983, D.C. Heath and Company), p. 1.

4. Ibid.

5. Christina Robb, "Who's Minding the Kids?" *Boston Globe Magazine*, March 3, 1985, pp. 27, 36. Reprinted courtesy of The Boston Globe.

6. S.J. Diamond, "Women on the Job: Surge Widely Felt," *Los Angeles Times*, September 9, 1984, p. 9.

7. Testimony at hearing before the Select Committee on Children, Youth, and Families, San Francisco, June 18, 1984, p. 49 of printed testimony (Washington, D.C.: U.S. Government Printing Office, 1985).

8. Maria L. La Ganga, "Experts Disagree—Child Care: Do Careers Pose Perils?" *Los Angeles Times*, September 16, 1984, sec. 1, p. 24. Copyright, 1984, Los Angeles Times. Reprinted by permission.

9. Reprinted by permission of the publisher, from Marian Blum, *The Day-Care Dilemma* (Lexington, Mass.: Lexington Books, D.C. Heath and Company, Copyright 1983, D.C. Heath and Company), p. 86.

10. Maria Crockett, "For Day Care, There's No Place like Home," *Christian Science Monitor*, April 16, 1984, p. 31.

11. Ibid.
12. Reprinted by permission of the publisher, from Marian Blum, *The Day-Care Dilemma* (Lexington, Mass.: Lexington Books, D.C. Heath and Company, Copyright 1983, D.C. Heath and Company), p. 87.
13. Marjorie Gelb, "Child Abuse: Benefits of Child Care Outweigh Parents' Fears," *Maine Sunday Telegram*, May 5, 1985, sec. A, p. 41.
14. Ibid.
15. Linda Burton, "What's a Smart Woman Like You Doing at Home?" *Christian Science Monitor*, December 7, 1982, "Speaking Out" column. Reprinted with permission of the author.
16. "What Price Day Care?" *Newsweek*, September 10, 1984, p. 21.
17. Ibid.
18. Marcy Whitebook et al., "Who's Minding the Child Care Workers?" *Newsweek*, July 23, 1983, p. 45, cited in Blum, *The Day-Care Dilemma*, p. 23. Reprinted by permission of the publisher, from Marian Blum, *The Day-Care Dilemma* (Lexington, Mass.: Lexington Books, D.C. Heath and Company, Copyright 1983, D.C. Heath and Company).
19. Letter in "Problems and Solutions," *Welcome Home*, January 1985, p. 23.
20. Dr. William Rodrigues, Children's Hospital, Washington, D.C., cited in Blum, *The Day-Care Dilemma*, p. 74. Reprinted by permission of the publisher, from Marian Blum, *The Day-Care Dilemma* (Lexington, Mass.: Lexington Books, D.C. Heath and Company, Copyright 1983, D.C. Heath and Company).
21. Testimony at hearings before the Select Committee on Children, Youth, and Families, by parents, community leaders, and day care workers. See printed testimony from April, June, and September 1984 hearings (Washington, D.C.: U.S. Government Printing Office, 1984, 1985).

4. CAN YOU REALLY *AFFORD* TO QUIT?

1. George Barbee, cited in Peter N. Spotts, "Adding a Child and Dropping an Income: A Time for Planning," *Christian Science Monitor*, May 18, 1984, p. B5.
2. Alvin Toffler, *The Third Wave* (New York: William Morrow, 1980), pp. 282–83.
3. Spotts, "Adding a Child," p. B6.
4. Cited in Shirley Sloan Fader, "A Guide to Part Time Work," *Ladies' Home Journal*, October 1984, p. 66.
5. "From a Single Mother at Home," *Welcome Home*, April 1984, p. 15.

5. SAVING MONEY INSTEAD OF MAKING IT

1. Mary Ann Cahill, *The Heart Has Its Own Reasons* (Franklin Park, Ill.: La Leche League International, 1983), p. 186.
2. Cahill, *The Heart*, pp. 107–08; italics mine.
3. Deborah Churchman, "Manufacturers Are Cranking Out Coupons by the Billions," *Christian Science Monitor*, January 10, 1984, Home and Family page.
4. Ibid.
5. Ibid.

6. Barbara Salsbury, with Cheri Loveless, *Cut Your Grocery Bills in Half!* (Washington, D.C.: Acropolis Books, 1983), p. 258.

6. HOW TO BE AS HAPPY AT HOME AS YOU'D HOPED TO BE

1. Lee Morical, *Where's My Happy Ending?* (Reading, Mass.: Addison-Wesley, 1984), p. 49.
2. Amitai Etzioni, telephone interview, December 17, 1985. See also comments in "The New One Paycheck Family," *Ladies' Home Journal,* September 1984, p. 89.
3. Linda Burton, "What Do You Do All Day?" *Welcome Home,* April 1984, p. 21.
4. Ibid., "A Place to Come Home To" *Welcome Home,* March 1984, p. 5.
5. Beth Bennett, "Homemakers' Survival Guide," *Woman's World,* May 7, 1985, p. 47.
6. Excerpts from Arlene Rossen Cardozo, *Woman at Home* (Garden City, N.Y.: Doubleday, 1970), p. 10. Copyright © 1970 by Arlene Rossen Cardozo. Reprinted by permission of Doubleday & Company, Inc.
7. Ibid., p. 2. Italics mine.
8. Janet Dittmer, "The Home Manager," *Welcome Home,* March 1984, p. 18.
9. Pat Cundick, "The Home Manager," *Welcome Home,* April 1985, p. 9.
10. Excerpt from Marilyn Gardner, "Cleaning Up the Original Family Business: How to Get Everybody into the Act," *Christian Science Monitor,* January 23, 1984, p. 21. Reprinted by permission from *The Christian Science Monitor,* © 1984, The Christian Science Publishing Society. All rights reserved.
11. Bonnie Watkins, "Entertaining Children on a Limited Budget," *Welcome Home,* April 1984, p. 8.
12. Blaine Taylor, *The Success Ethic and the Shattered American Dream* (Washington, D.C.: Acropolis Books, 1976), pp. 28–29.

7. BUILDING BRIDGES

1. Lee Morical, *Where's My Happy Ending?* (Reading, Mass.: Addison-Wesley, 1984), pp. 49–50.
2. Richard Nelson Bolles, *What Color Is Your Parachute?* (Berkeley, Calif.: 1976), p. i.
3. Marilyn Gardner, "Mother's Hours—Custom-tailoring the Workweek," *Christian Science Monitor,* September 12, 1985, p. 29. See also John Applegath, *Working Free: Practical Alternatives to the 9 to 5 Job* (New York: American Management Association, 1982).
4. Shirley Sloan Fader, "A Guide to Part Time Work," *Ladies' Home Journal,* October 1984, p. 72.
5. Deborah Churchman, "Getting Back into the Work Force—Without Going Back to School," *Christian Science Monitor,* December 15, 1983, p. 36.
6. Ibid.
7. Gretchen Olson Shively, "Occupation Housewife," *Mount Holyoke Alumnae Quarterly,* Summer 1982, p. 39.
8. Fader, "A Guide to Part Time Work," p. 66.
9. Naomi Barko, "The Part-Time Path," *Working Mother,* April 1985, pp. 38–39.
10. Caroline Bird in John Applegath, *Working Free,* p. i.

11. Quoted in Patricia Lee, *The Complete Guide to Job Sharing* (New York: Walker & Co., 1983), p. 92.
12. See Applegath, *Working Free*, p. 13, and Viviénne Sernaqué with Nachman Urieli, *Parttime Jobs* (New York: Ballantine Books, 1982), p. 20.
13. "From a Single Mother at Home," *Welcome Home*, April 1984, p. 15.
14. Tami Moore, "A New Direction," *New Beginnings*, March–April 1985, p. 44.

8. MAKING MONEY AT HOME, NAP TIME, NIGHTTIME, ANYTIME YOU CAN

1. Jaimie Day, cited in Barbara Evans Openshaw, "An Interior Design Business at Home," in "Making and Saving Money at Home" column, *Welcome Home*, August 1984, p. 25.
2. Georganne Fiumara, Mothers' Home Business Network promotional letter quoting from "A Dream Come True for Mothers Working at Home," *Woman*, February 1985.
3. Rushworth, M. Kidder, "The Flap over the Cottage-Industry Ban," *Christian Science Monitor*, December 12, 1983, p. 27.
4. Lynn Langway, et al., "'Worksteaders' Clean Up," *Newsweek*, January 9, 1984, p. 85.
5. Information from Sen. William Cohen, Portland, Maine, office, September, 1985.
6. Harley Shaiken, quoted on "CBS Evening News," December 3, 1984.
7. Debra Ann Hatten, "Where to Look for Nest Eggs to Hatch Your Enterprise Soundly," *Christian Science Monitor*, June 11, 1985, p. 27.
8. Phyllis Gillis, *Entrepreneurial Mothers* (New York: Rawson Associates, 1983), pp. 89–90.
9. Lynette Smith, cited in Barbara Evans Openshaw, "Lynette Smith: Home-Based Success," in "Making and Saving Money at Home" column, *Welcome Home*, June 1985, p. 19.
10. Langway, et al, "'Worksteaders' Clean Up," p. 87.
11. Pat Eggen, cited in *Homeworking Mothers: The Mothers' Home Business Network Newsletter*, ed. Georganne Fiumara, Spring 1985, p. 8.
12. Cynthia Harriman, personal interviews, November 1984 and April 1985.
13. Thomas Watterson, "The Keogh Plan, a Close Cousin of the IRA, Covers Any Kind of Self-employment Income," *Christian Science Monitor*, March 13, 1985, p. 21.

9. HOW MANY KIDS CAN RON AND NANCY CARE FOR IN THE WHITE HOUSE BASEMENT?

1. Jo Ann Gasper, Assistant for Social Services Policy, written statement submitted to hearing before Select Committee on Children, Youth, and Families, April 4, 1984, Washington, D.C., pp. 98–101 of printed testimony (Washington, D.C.: U.S. Government Printing Office, 1984).
2. Reprinted by permission of the publisher, from Marian Blum, *The Day-Care Dilemma* (Lexington Mass.: Lexington, Books, D.C. Heath and Company, Copyright 1983, D.C. Heath and Company), pp. 117–18.
3. Testimony at hearing before the Select Committee on Children, Youth, and Families, April 4, 1984, Washington, D.C., p. 29 of printed testimony (Washington, D.C.: U.S. Government Printing Office, 1984).

4. Testimony at hearing before the Select Committee on Children, Youth, and Families, May 21, 1984, Irving, Texas, p. 172 of printed testimony (Washington, D.C.: U.S. Government Printing Office, 1984).

5. Reprinted by permission of the publisher, from Marian Blum, *The Day-Care Dilemma* (Lexington, Mass.: Lexington Books, D.C. Heath and Company, Copyright 1983, D.C. Heath and Company), p. 42.

6. Ibid.

7. Testimony at hearing before the Select Committee on Children, Youth, and Families, May 21, 1984, Irving, Texas, pp. 139–43 of printed testimony (Washington, D.C.: U.S. Government Printing Office, 1984).

8. Excerpts from testimony before the Select Committee on Children, Youth, and Families (Washington, D.C.: Government Printing Office, 1984, 1985): from the May 21, 1984, Irving, Texas, hearing, p. 143; from the June 18, 1984, San Francisco hearing, p. 139; from the April 4, 1984, Washington, D.C., hearing, pp. 79–81.

9. Comments after hearing testimony before the Select Committee on Children, Youth, and Families, June 18, 1984, San Francisco (Washington, D.C.: U.S. Government Printing Office, 1985), p. 147.

10. "Additional Views," Select Committee on Children, Youth, and Families hearing, December 1983, Washington, D.C., (Washington, D.C.: U.S. Government Printing Office, 1984), pp. 82–84.

11. Eugene Steurle, cited by Daniel Patrick Moynihan, Godkin Lectures, Harvard University, April 8–9, 1985. Excerpt from *Family and Nation*, copyright © 1986 by Daniel Patrick Moynihan. Reprinted by permission of Harcourt Brace Jovanovich, Inc.

12. Excerpt from *Family and Nation*, copyright © 1986 by Daniel Patrick Moynihan. Reprinted by permission of Harcourt Brace Jovanovich, Inc.

13. Paul Blumberg, *Inequality in an Age of Decline* (New York: Oxford University Press, 1980), pp. 87–93.

14. Excerpt from *Family and Nation*, in press, copyright © 1986 by Daniel Patrick Moynihan. Reprinted by permission of Harcourt Brace Jovanovich, Inc.

15. Ibid.

16. Excerpt from *Family and Nation*, in press, copyright © by Daniel Patrick Moynihan. Reprinted by permission of Harcourt Brace Jovanovich, Inc.

17. Testimony at hearing before the Select Committee on Children, Youth, and Families, April 4, 1984, Washington, D.C., p. 26 of printed testimony (Washington, D.C.: U.S. Government Printing Office, 1984).

18. Testimony at hearing before the Select Committee on Children, Youth, and Families, June 18, 1984, San Francisco, p. 220 of printed testimony (Washington, D.C.: U.S. Government Printing Office, 1985).

19. Testimony at hearing before the Select Committee on Children, Youth, and Families, June 18, 1984, San Francisco, p. 127 of printed testimony (Washington, D.C.: U.S. Government Printing Office, 1985).

20. Testimony at hearing before the Select Committee on Children, Youth, and Families, April 4, 1984, Washington, D.C., p. 56 of printed testimony (Washington, D.C.: U.S. Government Printing Office, 1984).

21. Grace Mitchell, *The Day Care Book* (New York: Stein and Day, 1979), p. 230.

22. Lori Weinstein, cited in Marie Crockett, "For Day Care, There's No Place Like Home," *Christian Science Monitor*, April 16, 1984, p. 31.

23. "Additional Views," Select Committee on Children, Youth, and Families hearing, December 1983, Washington, D.C., (Washington, D.C.: U.S. Government Printing Office), p. 82.

24 D. Stanely Eitzen, *Social Problems*, 3rd ed. (Boston: Allyn & Bacon, in press).

25. Testimony at hearing before the Select Committee on Children, Youth, and Families, June 18, 1984, San Francisco, p. 60 of printed testimony (Washington, D.C.: U.S. Government Printing Office, 1985).

26. Figures are from the Congressional Budget Office and "Congress Watch," reported in Gregory Fossedal, "Corporate Welfare Out of Control," *The New Republic*, February 25, 1985, p. 17.

27. Ibid.

28. Richard D. Lamm, cited in Jeff B. Copeland, "Prof. Gloom's Pulpit," *Newsweek*, May 27, 1985, p. 30.

29. Michael Harrington, "Welfare: Time for Reform," *Saturday Review*, May 23, 1970, cited in Eitzen, *Social Problems*, in press.

10. CONCLUSION: MOVING BEYOND THE TRADITIONAL

1. Christine Compston, "From Stone Throwers to Hearth Tenders," lecture at the University of New Hampshire, Durham, N.H., July 14, 1982.

2. Ibid. See also William H. Chafe, *American Woman: Her Changing Social, Economic, and Political Roles, 1920–1974* (New York: Oxford University Press, 1974), and Carol Hymowitz and Michaele Weissman, *A History of Women in America* (New York: Bantam, 1978).

3. Chafe, *American Woman*, pp. 160–71.

4. Ibid.

5. Selma Fraiberg, *Every Child's Birthright: In Defense of Mothering*, cited in "Additional Views," Select Committee on Children, Youth, and Families hearing, December 1983, Washington, D.C. (Washington, D.C.: U.S. Government Printing Office), p. 83.

6. Maryann Brinley, "Let's End the War between Working and Staying-Home Mothers" in "The Mother's Page," *McCall's*, May 1985, p. 58.

7. Karen Levine, "Mother vs. Mother," *Parents*, June 1985, p. 64.

8. Reprinted by permission of the publisher, from Marian Blum, *The Day-Care Dilemma* (Lexington, Mass.: Lexington Books, D.C. Heath and Company, Copyright 1983, D.C. Heath and Company), p. 25.

9. Testimony at hearing before the Select Committee on Children, Youth, and Families, April 4, 1984, Washington, D.C., pp. 8–9 of printed testimony (Washington, D.C.: U.S. Government Printing Office, 1984).

10. Cheri Loveless, telephone interview, June 27, 1984.

11. Marilyn Gardner, "Advice to Today's Cinderellas: Fit Yourself for a Job, Not a Slipper," *Christian Science Monitor*, May 6, 1985, p. 41.

12. Edith B. Phelps, cited in Gardner, "Advice to Today's Cinderellas," p. 41.

13. Elaine Heffner, *Mothering: The Emotional Experience of Motherhood after Freud and Feminism* (Garden City, N.Y.: Doubleday, 1978), pp. 10–18.

14. Ibid., p. vi.

15. Lee Morical, *Where's My Happy Ending?* Reading, Mass.: Addison-Wesley, 1984), p. 104.

16. Shirley Sloan Fader, "A Guide to Part-time Work," *Ladies Home Journal*, October 1984, p. 72.
17. Alvin Toffler, *The Third Wave* (New York: William Morrow, 1980), pp. 216–19.
18. Linda Gray Sexton, *Between Two Worlds: Young Women in Crisis* (New York: William Morrow, 1979), p. 25.

Index

About the Author

C HRISTINE DAVIDSON was educated at Ripon College and Boston University and at the University of Exeter, Devon, England. She taught English in Boston public schools and was an instructor in nonfiction writing at Antioch-New England and the University of New Hampshire. She is now self-employed as a copyeditor and writer, concentrating on business, social, and women's issues. She lives in New Hampshire with her husband and two children.